FOREWORD BY EHUD BARA

RIDING THE WAVES

THE RISE AND FALL OF GEOTEK

BY

YARON EITAN
WITH URI MIRON

INKWATER
PRESS

To my wife Hagar, who rode out the stormy waves with me, and to my children, Nadav, Rotem and Noam, who make my life so very full.

My father told me once that few people have the chance to pursue their greatest vision and biggest dream, but even fewer get to see their career recover after their life project has failed. Over the years, he followed my stormy career with strong support and admiration. Unfortunately, he did not get to read this book, as he became ill and passed away in March, 2004. I am sure he would have been proud seeing my story go to print.

TABLE OF CONTENTS

FOREWORD

by Ehud Barak

"Riding The Waves: The Rise And Fall Of Geotek" tells the story of a remarkable company that came out of nowhere, it seemed, to adapt advanced Israeli military technology for the global wireless market. It attempted to do what few technology start-ups try: market its technology, in one of the most competitive arenas of its day, directly to consumers. And though Geotek ultimately did not succeed, it remains a powerful example of the importance of vision in entrepreneurship.

I have known Yaron for many years now, and followed Geotek's roller coaster ride, through its triumphs and its defeats, with great interest. In recent years, I have also done business with him personally, in the context of SCP Private Equity Partners, an investment firm in which he is a partner. There too, I had the opportunity to witness his passion for technological innovation and entrepreneurship.

"Riding The Waves" provides a fascinating glimpse into a true pioneer of the 1990s wireless revolution, a company that had the audacity to go up against some of the biggest, best-funded players in an incredibly competitive market. It tells the story of an entrepreneur who pursued an unlikely dream and, daring to risk failure, came closer to success than most would have thought possible.

INTRODUCTION

Over the last twenty years, I have had a good deal of professional success. In different roles, I met or exceeded goals set forth both by investors and by myself. I founded and built companies, managed existing ones through the good times and the bad, and sold businesses at great profit to all the parties involved. The story recounted in this book, however, is not of one of these successes.

The tale of Geotek Communications, and of my role as its founder and CEO, is ultimately one of failure. Geotek, after all, was a company forced to file for Chapter 11 Bankruptcy Protection and sell itself in parts. I, as the man who ran it, was responsible for my part in allowing that to happen. The fact that I was also the one who created Geotek, and led it to its earlier successes, was of little comfort to the investors who lost their money, the employees who were let go, or the customers whose wireless phones suddenly became useless. As a member of all these groups, I did understand the bitter feelings instigated by Geotek's downfall, although I certainly do not claim to be the victim in this story.

Why, then, did I decide to document this period of my life? Why expound on my greatest failure? The reason, quite simply, is that Geotek was my greatest failure, in the very best sense of the word. It was an extraordinary company that had the tenacity, the sheer impudence, to pursue a vision so ambitious that no established telecommunications company had ever attempted anything like it. Though it did not make it, its accomplishments were quite real.

First and foremost among these was the revolutionary technology that Geotek developed and introduced to the world of commercial cellular. From as early as 1992, years before the Internet became a household name, we had the foresight to understand that communications was moving in the direction of integration and convergence of all types of data. Geotek set out to develop technologies that would support not only digital networks, still a rarity at this time, but also digital *data* networks. As a result, during the brief period that Geotek's American networks were in service, they allowed for Internet-type features that would not be offered by other wireless carriers for many years to come. These included two-way text messaging, mobile credit-card verification and real-time map-based GPS functionality. Combined with our push-to-talk and telephony offerings, these applications significantly improved productivity for many of our customers. These companies, such as Airborne Express, Time Warner Cable and Pepsi, could suddenly communicate in a very meaningful way with their mobile employees *while they were doing their primary job of driving.* From a single desktop workstation, an operator could supervise and direct an entire fleet. Furthermore, the workstation could be tied into other corporate applications on the network, thereby eliminating a great deal of administrative overhead.

It is a mark of the fundamental strength of Geotek's core technology that, to this day, the vast majority of cellular networks throughout the world are capable of only a fraction of the capacity, per MHz of spectrum, that we were able to offer when we launched our American service almost eight years ago.

To finance its ambitious vision, Geotek raised a total of over $800M. During the late 1990s, that sum would come to seem almost ordinary. At the time it was raised, however, it constituted an unusually high level of investment for a technology start-up, especially one whose research and development activities were based in Israel, and therefore vulnerable to political instabilities in the Middle East. Geotek's love affair with Wall Street was not as it seemed, however. The relationship was turbulent and ultimately contributed as much to the company's collapse as it did to its ability to rapidly grow.

Along with the big ambitions and big money came the need to create a big organization. Geotek grew rapidly but piecemeal. As with so many other start-ups, inability to manage expectations and effectively predict the company's needs turned Geotek into a sprawling organization, at one time numbering over 1,200 employees, located throughout the United States, Israel, the UK, Canada, Germany and South Korea. Further adding to the organizational challenges was the significant number of strategic partnerships, both big and small, into which Geotek entered. Theses included partnerships with companies such as IBM, Hughes Electronics, Mitsubishi, Hyundai and, most complicated of all, Rafael, the Israeli government-owned defense company that developed the core communication technology Geotek utilized.

The story of Geotek is one from which every aspiring entrepreneur can learn. It is, above all, a story about what it takes to pursue a great but unlikely ambition. It is the tale of a management team that presided over the development and implementation of revolutionary technology that was years

ahead of its time. We encountered so many seemingly impen-
etrable obstacles that I sometimes find myself amazed at how
close we came to making it after all. For all but the last few
months, I was at the very center of Geotek, for better and for
worse. This book presents my recollections not only of the
great adventure that Geotek was, but also of the lessons I
learned the hard way during my years of leading it.

RIDING THE WAVES

CHAPTER ONE
COMING TO PHILADELPHIA

I arrived in the United States on a hot summer day in 1982. After landing at JFK, I took a cab to Penn Station and boarded a train to Philadelphia. In a few weeks, I was to start a PhD program at the University of Pennsylvania's Wharton School of Business. I was looking forward to this with a mixture of excitement and trepidation, the latter a result of my knowledge that I really could not afford such an expensive education.

America is a remarkable change of scenery for nearly every newcomer, but it was especially so in my case. I had only just completed a sixty-day stint as a reserve officer for the Israeli Defense Force. The military was engaged in a highly unpopular war in Lebanon back then, and a sense of gloom and lack of direction was permeating through Israeli society. At 25, I had spent over five years as an officer in an elite infantry unit and three years in the reserves. I enjoyed my years in the IDF far more than the time I spent afterwards getting a BA in Economics from Haifa University. The years in the military had a big impact on my personality and character. I have always felt that my time in the infantry made me develop a more calm and balanced view of life, one in which nothing, including myself, was taken too seriously. Life as a military officer was so rewarding that I seriously considered following in my father's footsteps and becoming a career military man. The only possible path that appealed to me more was to go to school in the U.S., an option which my father, David, strongly encouraged. It was not that I was unimpressed with the level of studies in Israel, but rather that I knew that studying business in the United States would be something completely different. Simply *being* there would. It would mean leaving behind all that was ordinary and mundane, everything with which I was so very familiar.

Well, almost everything. I had limited my search of schools to ones that were located in the Philadelphia area. My uncle, Zvi Muscal, was a successful banker in the city, and while I was planning to rent an apartment as soon as I arrived, I did prefer to live as close as possible to some family. It was only because I was looking in such a small area that I even applied to Wharton. All I knew about it was that it was the University of Pennsylvania's business school. It was not until the fall semester started that I realized it was far more prestigious, not to mention selective, than any other school in the university. I suspect Wharton accepted me mainly because I seemed like an interesting character, a guy with a bunch of glowing but rather poorly written letters of recommendation from infantry officers in the Israeli Military. Looking back, I suspect I came across in my application as much more confident than I had any reason to be. Chances are, that attitude contributed as much to my acceptance as anything else. It was not that I was arrogant; I simply had not done enough research to know I was applying to a school that was in such demand. I had done just enough research, however, to realize that with my dismal scores in the Verbal section of the GMAT, I would stand a better chance of being accepted if I applied for the PhD track rather than the more sought-after MBA program. I had only a vague idea of the differences between the two, but I was soon to find out.

September 7th, 1982, marked the first day of classes – and my first day as an "aspiring" academic in "theoretical business administration." The only problem was, it was not who I was or what I wanted to be. I had gotten a B.A. in economics because it seemed like a practical field to study. Like most economics undergraduates, however, I had no wish to become one of the graduate students that one sees so often in economics departments throughout the world, discussing statistical methods, quantitative analysis and other such esoteric topics. I came to school in the U.S. because I wanted to learn the skills necessary to become a successful businessman in the real world. One of the finest places to be trained in them, unfortunately, turned out to be the classroom next door...

My unhappiness with the program I had chosen, however, was a less urgent concern than the fact that I was soon in real danger of flunking out altogether. Though my grades would improve dramatically over time, my academic performance during those first months of the fall semester was quite worrisome. I had never before had to stress too much about grades, as I always seemed to do well enough, and a 4.0 GPA was not something I dreamed about anyway. Now, however, I was in trouble. I was simply under-prepared for the rigors of a Wharton curriculum, let alone its PhD version. My English, while more or less adequate for everyday conversation, was just embarrassing in the context of graduate-level papers. Even reading assignments required hours of deciphering unfamiliar words with the help of a dictionary. Contributing to these difficulties was the fact that, unlike in Wharton's MBA program, there were almost no foreign students pursuing a PhD.

This increased my relative disadvantage and, even more importantly, my feeling of isolation from my classmates, who, while about the same age as I, seemed to have little experience of the real world. The small size of my classes made it all the more difficult to blend in, since everyone always seemed to be aware of everybody else's presence. Part of my dissatisfaction was my own fault, as I am the type of person who tends to say whatever is on his mind, even when unsure. Many people appreciate this straightforwardness, but it did not garner too much respect in my research-oriented courses where precision was highly prized.

It became apparent to me early in the semester that I had made a terrible mistake by applying to the PhD program. To make matters worse, the more time I spent on campus, the more I realized how wonderful the Wharton *MBA* program was. Living in America was costing more than I had expected, and the prospect of wasting my life's savings on an education that seemed so pointless made me realize that I had to do something. I even flirted with the idea of dropping out, and it is possible I would have swallowed my pride and done so were it not for the one bright spot in my life during this period: my job for the Israeli Consulate.

With a war raging in Lebanon, and increasing tensions between Israel and the Palestinians, the period in which I came to the U.S. was one of intense criticism of Israel throughout the world. The then-recent peace deal with Egypt, brokered by President Jimmy Carter at Camp David, had tied Israel to the United States closer than ever before, both financially and strategically. Public perception of Israel in America was therefore of great concern to the Israeli government, and its local diplomatic corps' public relations role took on more urgency than ever before.

An acquaintance of mine in the Philadelphia Consulate, upon learning that I was coming to study at Wharton, suggested that I try out for a job as a sponsored guest speaker. If accepted, I would be added to a list of "preferred speakers" that the Consulate disseminated to local organizations, both Jewish and non-Jewish, that were seeking guest lecturers to speak about Israel-related issues. The job paid an honorarium of $25-$100 per engagement, which was a significant amount of money for me given that the studio I had rented, which was rundown but close to campus, cost just $220 a month. A few invitations on even a semi-regular basis could thus pay for a good chunk of my living expenses. It was income I desperately needed if I were to make it through my entire studies.

I have always been a confident and comfortable public speaker, so after my first trial engagement went well, I was accepted into the program and placed on the Consulate's preferred speaker list. The list included a wide variety of speakers, from the Consul himself down to minor war veterans such as myself (needless to say, not everyone was available for every occasion). Ironically, perhaps, my lack of awareness of the extent to which my English was lacking, which accounted for much of my difficulties in school, actually helped in the context of the speaking engagements I was doing on the side. Had I realized how I sounded to a native English-speaking audience, I would have been so mortified I might have lost my confidence. As it was, the fact that I believed in what I was saying, and that I enjoyed saying it, made the way I spoke far less important. Ultimately, the reason the speeches were successful was that the audience had become engaged. It was my first real-world example of an important principal of marketing: one can never just sell one's product, but must always sell him- or herself as well. Whether the product is cellular service or a major stake in the company that provides it, the most important aspect of a sales pitch, short of the product itself, is the presenter's ability to engage the audience. If they are not excited, if they are not, at least on some level, *enjoying* themselves, than a valuable opportunity has been wasted, even if the outcome of the meeting, in the immediate term, is successful.

While the consulate job provided me with income and, equally as important, a sense that I was doing something valuable and worthwhile, I was still primarily occupied with my dissatisfaction at school. Having quickly realized that the PhD was not for me, I decided to try to transfer to Wharton's MBA program. In an effort to improve my grades, I hired a typist at $2 per page to type my papers and, in the process, correct my most egregious grammatical errors. I could not really afford this additional expense, but since the courses I was taking did not have tests, I knew that improving the quality of my papers was crucial to showing that I had the potential to succeed in the MBA program.

I also realized, however, that even if my grades did improve, that by itself would not convince the pertinent admissions committee to allow me to transfer. Since the PhD program was so much less selective than the MBA, there was a natural suspicion whenever a transfer was requested that the original application had been insincere, that the applicant had meant from the beginning to use the PhD program as a back door into the MBA. Nevertheless, I felt that I had to try. Since my uncle had a friend who was a professor at Wharton, I started by trying to convince him. Ultimately, he probably did not have much influence on the committee's decision, but he did help point me towards the right people and provided me with valuable advice on approaching them. My transfer request slowly made its way through the bureaucratic process, and making sure that it moved forwards consumed a good deal of my time during that first semester. Eventually, I was granted permission to switch from the PhD to the MBA program. I suspect that, in the end, what tipped the balance in my favor was the fact that most of my teachers had come to believe that I did have an aptitude for business and that it would be better served in the more hands-on MBA program.

Having been given full credit for my PhD courses, as MBA electives, I finally began, in late January of 1983, the type of business studies I imagined when I had first applied to Wharton. The next year and a half was gratifying on both an academic and social level. The majority of my courses featured little of the theory I had come to resent during the first semester. They were filled, instead, with case studies and examples of real life business techniques. I found myself enjoying not only obvious subjects, such as management and marketing, but also others like financing and operations. Equally as valuable, however, was the interaction with the MBA student population, with whom I had far more in common than with the PhD students. I also became very involved with the Jewish and Israeli groups at the school. Many of the connections I made during this period later proved to be real assets both professionally and personally.

As the second year began and my classmates were returning with stories about their summer internships, I assumed I would be going back to Israel after the year ended. Though my grades had improved, they were hardly extraordinary, and since I did not have a Green Card, it was unlikely that an American company would hire me. This reality did not trouble me too much, however, as I had never planned to stay in the U.S permanently. While it would have been nice to gain some work experience in America, it was not something that I wanted passionately, and I pursued the matter only casually.

Early in the second year, I was invited, as a result of one of my uncle's connections, to a meeting at the Greater Philadelphia Chamber of Commerce. This was a non-profit organization, sponsored by major corporations in the area, whose mission was to promote local economic growth. At the meeting, I was told that the Chamber of Commerce, along with the American Jewish Committee (AJC), was in the process of forming a new program aimed at encouraging economic cooperation between companies based in the Delaware Valley area and Israeli companies. The new organization, to be called The Philadelphia-Israel Economic Development Committee, was still very much at an early stage of formation and it needed an executive director to build some of the infrastructure and run its day-to-day operations. To my utter surprise, the representatives of the Chamber of Commerce and the AJC offered the position to me.

Since I was still at school, I began working for the Philadelphia-Israel Economic Development Committee as a part-time employee. The Chamber of Commerce and the AJC had quickly assembled a board of advisors that included some of the most successful Jewish figures in the Philadelphia business community. The AJC also supplied the committee with office space and secretarial support, so we faced few of the logistical problems often encountered by new non-profit organizations.

My work revolved mainly around setting up conferences and presentations and acting as a matchmaker of sorts between Philadelphia businessmen and their Israeli counterparts. It was not the most exciting or challenging work, but it did provide me with an introduction, at least on a shallow level, to a variety of local businesses and some of their highest-level executives.

At around the same time that I was offered the job for the Israel-Philadelphia Committee, I met a new student at Wharton, there for just a one-year Sabbatical, by the name of Yoram Oron. Yoram was an employee of Koor, one of the largest Israeli corporations. Though we had never met back in Israel, we did share a number of acquaintances, since my father also worked for Koor at the time.

Yoram showed a great deal of interest in my work for the Israel-Philadelphia Committee, and since I was eager to hear about the business situation in Israel, we had plenty to talk about and got along quite well. Nevertheless, I was completely unprepared for a proposal he made to me one day early in my last semester of school. He had been planning to leave Koor and start a technology company for some time, he told me. In fact, he already had a business plan as well as two partners, both of whom, though young, were bright and well qualified. Like himself, however, neither had quit their job yet and their plans were still under wraps. What they needed to make the new company a reality, he said, was enough financing to cover the initial cost of setting up offices and developing the proposed product, a highly specialized electrical fuze for artillery and mortar shells. The new company was to be named Reshef, after the Hebrew word for muzzle flash (or sparks).

It was as much a testament to Yoram's naivety as it was to my great fortune that he then offered me a position, straight out of business school, as an equal partner in his new venture. My job, at least in the beginning, would be to raise about $2M in the U.S. (there was almost no venture capital available in Israel at the time). Though the figure seemed an astronomical amount to raise, given that I had virtually no business experience at all, I gladly accepted the offer.

Over the next few months, Yoram and I spent much of our time working on his business plan. Though it was quite a promising and well-thought-out proposal, it needed to be made more marketable if we were to use it to raise capital from American investors.

Between my work with Yoram and my obligations to the Israel-Philadelphia Committee, schoolwork had become a smaller concern for me as I neared the end of my studies. Soon after graduation, Yoram returned to Israel and began laying the groundwork for the as-yet-unnamed new company. He was joined by our two other partners, Moshe Rotem, an operations man, and Zohar Zisapel, an electronics engineer and entrepreneur who would later become one of the leading figures of Israel's high-technology industry. I, meanwhile, remained in the United States with the task of raising more money than I had ever seen.

CHAPTER TWO

FROM RESHEF TO GEOTEK

Soon after I accepted Yoram's offer of becoming his partner, I contacted Steven Goodman, an attorney who had been warmly recommended by one of my contacts at the Philadelphia-Israel Economic Development Committee. My consultations with Steven confirmed for me something that I had already suspected - that given the partners' relative youth and inexperience, our best chance of raising the kind of money we needed was through the private placement of equity.

In 1984, the venture capital industry, which would grow to dominate technological entrepreneurship throughout the world in subsequent decades, was still in its infancy. Although it would soon establish itself as *the* model for startup financing, it had yet to overshadow the more traditional technique of directly selling small amounts of equity to wealthy private investors. These investors typically differed from venture capital funds in two major ways - they had significantly less money to invest (on an individual basis), and were far less sophisticated.

The concept of raising capital with Research and Development Tax Shelters was quite fashionable in the 1980s. High-income individuals, who were paying income taxes at a marginal rate of over 60%, were eager to shelter some of their earnings in risky R&D partnerships. With Steven's help, I created a limited partnership that would allow our investors to take advantage of these tax benefits. The goal of raising $2M, on which Yoram and I had settled, meant I would need to convince dozens of investors to invest in our new company. The sums involved needed to be low enough that I could target a wide variety of investors. If units were priced too low, however, the process would take forever, and by the time it was over, we could have lost much of our momentum back in Israel. After some consultation with Steven, I decided on a price of $50,000 a unit (though I did agree to issue "half-units" on several occasions). Since the unit represented an interest in a limited partnership as well as a share of Reshef, the limited partnership interest could be treated as an expense by investors.

During one of our first meetings, Steven offered to introduce me to one of his clients, a man by the name of Dick Samuel. Dick Samuel was a New Jersey based patent lawyer who had just one client – the publicly traded Patlex corporation, of which he was President and CEO. Patlex's sole asset at the time was the ownership of the disputed patents of Dr. Gordon Gould, a brilliant scientist who, back in the late 50s, had discovered some of the earliest and most widely used lasers, including the gas lasers and solid state lasers. Though he had patented the lasers, Gould had not seen a cent from the profits his inventions generated, as his patents were being infringed by dozens of companies worldwide. For decades, his struggle to have the patents enforced received little support, largely due to his rumored ties to communist organizations. In the late 70s, however, he was discovered by Kenneth Langon, owner of the Wall Street firm Invemed, who realized the enormous financial potential in Gould's claims. Langon convinced Dick Samuel, who was already representing Gould by then, to leave his firm and come work exclusively on Gould's case. To fund the court fights, Langon took over the shell of a public company, renamed it Patlex, and used it to raise money from the public. By the time I met Dick Samuel, Patlex had already been in existence for four or five years, and though it had yet to win a single court battle, its valuation had risen to about $100M. While the confidence of the investing public gave the company the ability to wage expensive court fights, it also made the stock extremely risky to own. Langon and Dick Samuel knew that a major court defeat could set the share's price tumbling. To protect Patlex from this scenario, they had recently started looking to diversify its holdings, in the hope of cushioning the blow from a potential adverse legal ruling.

When I showed Dick Samuel our business plan and told him about our financing situation (or lack thereof), he quickly came up with a rather outrageous proposition. Patlex would *loan* us a quarter of a million dollars, he offered, in exchange for an immediate one third stake in Reshef. The loan was to be paid back once the rest of the $2M was secured, at which point Patlex would have its shares diluted, along with those of the four original partners, in order to accommodate the new investors I had found. Additionally, Dick Samuel and Langon would also try to help me find additional investors. Though it was a pretty lousy deal, from a financial standpoint, it was the best and only offer I had received thus far, and it had the potential to raise our level of credibility with investors, which I knew could be very helpful. Thus, after consulting with Steven, Yoram (who was still in the U.S.) and the partners in Israel, I accepted Dick Samuel's offer. Almost overnight, Patlex became our biggest shareholder. With the money from the loan, Yoram was able to start laying the groundwork for Reshef as soon as he returned to Israel in the summer of 1984.

Langon and Dick Samuel stuck to their word and introduces me to several wealthy individuals I likely would not have been able to obtain meetings with otherwise. Among these were Bernie Marcus, founder of Home Depot, who agreed to invest $100K in Reshef, and three wealthy Jewish real-estate developers in New Jersey, each of whom wound up investing $50K-$100K. The majority of the investors brought on board, however, came through my own contacts, or those of personal acquaintances who helped me out with leads. All told, I spent nine months crisscrossing the United States and meeting with potential sources of financing. The only common trait among the individuals I met, other than the fact that they had money to invest, was that the vast majority of them were Jewish. This was hardly due to a preference for non-gentile money, but was the natural result of two main circumstances. Firstly, many of my contacts came from the Philadelphia-Israel Economic Development Committee, which was naturally a Jewish-oriented organization. Secondly, the fact that the venture I was pitching was based in Israel raised the acceptable risk threshold for those investors who felt passionate about the country and were attracted by the idea of killing two birds with one stone. The key to attracting such investors was to understand that while they were not looking to make philanthropic gifts, they did feel a powerful incentive to make an investment that also contributed to their cause. It was a potent illustration of the role of emotion for many investors, and an extremely valuable learning experience for me.

The period I spent raising funds, much of it on the road, in parts of the country that I had never before visited, was as exhausting as it was rewarding. I was my entire organization, and the motel room was my office. Finding out that I could effectively function under these conditions made me realize, in a profound way, that I had made the right decision by accepting Yoram's offer and becoming an "accidental" entrepreneur. As it turned out, the small fund raising I conducted for Reshef marked the beginning of a long career raising far greater amounts of capital.

Less than a year after graduation, I found myself a partner in a technology startup that had real money to pursue its vision. Altogether, I had successfully raised $2.1M in investments, slightly exceeding the difficult goal that Yoram and I had agreed on back in school. By the time I returned to Israel, in early 1985, the money was already being used on the ground, mainly for the research and development of our first product line. Reshef was now, at least potentially, a contender in its field.

Upon my return, I assumed the role of CFO and Vice-President of Business Development at Reshef. Because the focus of the company was now on development, my position was much less demanding than it had been in the U.S. Yoram and I had expected this might be the case, and had therefore agreed that I would work for Reshef on a part-time basis. The rest of my time was spent working for Patlex, which had offered me a job as its representative in Israel. The position entailed searching for potential investments and, once such investments had been made, being Patlex's local point man for all issues regarding the companies in question. In essence, it was a form of venture capital management, a field to which I would return, under very different circumstances, many years later.

Between 1985-1987, Patlex made two major investments in Israel. The first was the purchase of Oram Electrical

Industries, a small, privately held manufacturer of electrical transformers that was located in the Tel-Aviv suburb of Ramla. Shortly after the acquisition, I convinced my father, David Eitan, to leave his job as the CEO of Carmel Forge, a Koor Company and come run Oram. Largely because of his involvement, the company was quite successful in those years, especially once it had secured a major contract from the Israeli branch of IBM. Bringing my father on board gave me the rare opportunity to work with him, which was a great experience for both of us. There are mixed opinions about working with close family members, but I think the situation's positive aspects are too often overlooked. I worked with my father when I was young and inexperienced in the business world, and later on I worked with my uncle, Shalom Eitan, in some of the most critical years for Geotek. I believe that if family members behave maturely when working together, the level of trust and familiarity that their personal relationship brings to the table is of enormous benefit. I can only hope that I will be lucky enough to work with my own children some day.

The second Israeli investment Patlex made was the financing of a joint venture with Israel's Nuclear Center in the southern city of Dimona, where the country's alleged nuclear weapons program is centered. The company, which we named Rotlex (an amalgam of ROTEM, the Nuclear Center's commercial division, and Patlex), developed the Center's technology in the field of nondestructive testing. Though it had limited success, it remains in existence to this day, much to my surprise.

At Reshef, I became increasingly involved in sales as the development of our first product progressed. Much of the early orders came from the Israeli Defense Force, with which Yoram had worked in the past. A smaller portion came from countries in South America, where I traveled several times.

Early in 1987, I attended a meeting of Patlex's board of directors in New York City. As was often the case, I was wearing my two hats at the same time, giving the board my reports both as a Patlex employee and as the representative of Reshef. In this case, it was the latter report that proved to be the more significant one. Somehow, between the IDF and international orders, Reshef had made $10M worth of advanced sales, all before it had shipped a single fuze. Patlex's board, which was still looking for ways to diversify, was naturally impressed with these results. Still, it came as a complete shock to me when Tom Marques, a board member who had been the CFO of Ross Perot's EDS, suggested that Patlex simply acquire Reshef. Even more surprising, however, was that most of the other board members seemed to support the idea as well. Though no numbers were mentioned in that meeting, it was clear that, if the acquisition did go through, it would be at a very favorable price for Reshef's investors.

Over the next few months, I negotiated with Patlex a stock buyout deal that valued Reshef at approximately $16M. Roughly half of that amount was to be split between Yoram, Moshe, Zohar and myself, though we would be permitted to sell only a few hundred thousand dollars worth of stock immediately. As the negotiations drew to a close, however, Dick Samuel called me to make another request. Patlex's board members, he said, had become nervous about his ability to oversee the company's growing number of industrial holdings on top of its patent claims. As a result, they were having second thoughts about purchasing Reshef. What he needed in order to convince them to seal the deal, he told me, was for me to agree to come back to America for a year and help him run the day-to-day operations of Patlex.

I was approaching the age of 30 around this time, and was starting to seriously consider settling down. I discussed Dick Samuel's request with Hagar, my girlfriend, who was a first year Masters' student at Haifa University back then. We had spoken about getting married before, but Dick's request made everything more urgent. Accepting Patlex's offer was a difficult decision to make, but ultimately I felt it had to be done if I did not want the Reshef deal to be jeopardized. As a result, Hagar and I left for the U.S. that July, a week after we were wed. It was a wonderful career move for me, but a huge sacrifice for Hagar, who gave up many of her personal and professional dreams to support my own. So often, those of us in the business world fail to acknowledge the heavy price paid by our spouses as we pursue our ambitions. If given the opportunity to live my life over again, I would not have asked Hagar to give up as much as she did.

———~·.·~———

By this point, Patlex had relocated to Los Angeles, moving into the offices of Apollo Laser, a manufacturer of laser equipment that it had recently purchased. Once Hagar and I had settled in, I began working closely with Dick Samuel on all aspects of Patlex's operations, which could be classified into two main types. The first, and most important of the two, remained the pursuit of restitution and licensing fees from parties that had violated laser patents owned by Patlex. The second part of the company's operations, however, the overseeing of its industrial portfolio – which now included Reshef, Oram, Rotlex and Apollo Laser – accounted for an increasing portion of our day-to-day activities.

I had only committed to staying in the U.S. for a period of one year. Several months before that time was to end, however,

Dick Samuel asked the board of directors to appoint me President and COO. It was a major professional promotion, and it convinced me to stay. The opportunity to become president of a company the size of Patlex while still in my early 30s was simply too good to pass up.

In early 1988, Patlex won its first major patent infringement lawsuit, against a company in Florida called Control Laser Corporation. The $10M judgment essentially gave us full control of the company, since Control Laser, which had no way of coming up with that kind of money, was forced to issue new stocks and hand them over Patlex. With the company in great distress, and its valuation very low, the number of shares it had to issue us was greater than the total number of its outstanding shares had been prior to the judgment. Within a few months, we sold our controlling stake of Control Laser to Quantronix, a Long Island based laser company.

The judgment against Control Laser proved to be a watershed moment for Patlex, both because of its legal incisiveness and because of the fact that few wanted to risk sharing Control Laser's fate. It set a precedent that eventually forced nearly every major manufacturer of the types of lasers patented by Gordon Gould decades earlier to settle with Patlex. Though these settlements sometimes involved restitution, their more crucial aspect was a commitment to licensing the technology that the manufacturers had for years insisted was in the public domain. The Control laser judgment was the kind of victory that the financial markets, which had supported Langon and Dick Samuel's crusade for nearly a decade, had been eagerly anticipating.

Shortly after the judgment, certain tensions that had been bubbling up in the background for some time at Patlex began coming to the fore. At the center of these were differences, in both personal style and corporate vision, between Langon, Patlex's founder and biggest shareholder, and Dick Samuel, the company's CEO and Chairman of the Board. As a result of these differences, Dick Samuel was forced to resign from his managerial positions, remaining only a member of the board. His replacement, a candidate supported enthusiastically by Langon, was Col. Frank Borman, a former Apollo astronaut and the former head of Eastern Airlines. Though Borman was certainly a high profile and well-qualified individual to bring on board, his work at Patlex was very part-time. Typically, he would fly in once a week from his home in Las Cruces, New Mexico, I would pick him up from Van-Nuys Airport, and we would spend most of the day going over the past week's major issues. Though we were in close contact during other times as well, I effectively handled most of the day-to-day duties. Still, I had very good working relationship with Borman and considered it an honor to work with him.

One of the more bewildering chapters in my Patlex career began with a 7:00 AM phone call one day in early 1989. It was from an Israeli employee, who told me, in an urgent whisper, to come to the office right away. Before I could ask any questions, he was forced to hang up. When I reached the office a short time later, the parking lot, which was normally almost empty at that hour, was filled with cars. Upon entering the building, I was swarmed by Federal agents, their badges flashing, who demanded that I produce the key to our storage space. This space had not been used for as long as I had been working in the office, and it took some time before I was able to locate the key. As I was searching for it, the agents informed me that they belonged to the L.A. branch of the Commerce Department, and that they were under no obligation to reveal the nature or reason for their investigation. Once the empty storage space was opened, about half of the twenty or so agents proceeded to search it, while the rest began hauling files and conducting interviews with employees.

As months passed and the investigation dragged on, it began to have a serious impact on some of Patlex's industrial activities. Particularly hurt was Reshef, which purchased some of the components for its fuzes in the U.S. Since Reshef had essentially become an American company when it was acquired by Patlex, it was required to obtain export licenses for the American components it bought for use in Israel. These licenses were issued by the Office of Munitions Control at the State Department. The Commerce Department investigation, however, automatically placed Reshef on a list of companies refused licenses. Patlex's repeated requests that an exception be made only seemed to make the Commerce Department more suspicious, as it began to investigate Yoram Oron as well.

The legal expenses associated with the investigation were quite high. Since the Commerce Department would not reveal the subject of its investigation, Patlex's board hired an independent council to go over its books and try to figure out if it had somehow broken the law. Although this in-house inquiry produced no results, it cost Patlex over a million dollars. In addition, many of the company's officers, including myself, were forced to retain private attorneys as well.

Several months after the investigation began, Patlex hired a lobbyist in Washington, DC, who was able to arrange meetings for me with several members of Congress, including Sen. Joseph Lieberman of Connecticut and Rep. Bernie Frank of Massachusetts. With their help, I was able to obtain a meeting with the Deputy Director of the Office of Munitions Control, who told me that he himself had no idea what the reason for the Commerce Department's investigation was. He agreed, however, to make the continued withholding of Reshef's export permits contingent on the Commerce Department providing his office with more information on the nature of its investigation. When it failed to do so, the export licenses were unceremoniously restored, much to the relief of everyone at Reshef.

By mid 1989, Patlex had signed multi-year licensing deals for its laser technologies with over a hundred companies worldwide. Though the value of these contracts was not as high as some had predicted, it was nevertheless quite significant. Collectively, they were expected to yield $10M-$15M annually for years to come.

With Patlex's laser patents now a huge source of cash flow, rather than legal expenses, it had little need for the various industrial companies it owned. As the on-going investigation by the Commerce department showed, they had the potential to be a real source of unwanted distraction. More importantly, there was a growing sentiment among the major shareholders that the company should search for new investments that would provide it with a way of sheltering itself from at least some of the high taxes it was paying. The Board of Directors decided, therefore, to spin off Patlex's industrial holdings in their entirety. Since I had been brought on mainly to oversee these companies, I was the natural choice for CEO of the spun-off corporation. Patlex agreed to provide the new company, which would own Reshef, Oram, Apollo Lasers and Rotlex, $1.5M to cover its initial operating costs. After that, we would be on our own, cut off from Patlex's vast cash reserves.

A few years earlier, before Reshef had become part of Patlex, we had formed a subsidiary called Geotech to sell fuzes in South America. The name had stuck with me, and I decided to use it for the new company, which would now own Reshef. I changed the "ch" to a "k" because it made the name sound more interesting to me. Since the spun-off company was essentially a small holding company, I added the word "Industries" at the end as well (it would later be changed to "Communications").

I was now in the odd position of being, among other things, the boss of the man who had given me my first big break, Yoram Oron.

CHAPTER THREE

SEARCHING FOR A DIRECTION

To say that the newly spun-off Geotek was an "unsexy" company would be a major understatement. To the extent that Patlex's shareholder were represented by their Board of Directors, most of them wanted as little to do with Geotek's properties as possible. The spin-off had been amicable, but its underlying motivation was clear to all – the industrial companies Patlex had acquired over the years had outgrown their usefulness. Those investors who had placed a bet on Dr. Gould's laser patents wanted to be in the royalty collection business, with its 100% profit margins, not in the business of manufacturing and selling "widgets" of one type or another. This was reflected in Geotek's stock price, which, from 1989 through the early 1990s, went nowhere but down (the stock began trading at around $2 a share, and dropped to a low of $1 over time).

My first order of business after the spin-off was to come up with a business plan for Geotek, to determine what to do, exactly, with its various unrelated parts. Since most of our holdings were in Israel, I decided to adopt a typical business model used by Israeli-American companies. Geotek would continue doing Research and Development in Israel while it worked to leverage its presence in the U.S., and its status as a publicly traded American company, to improve sales in the vast domestic market. It was a model that had worked for many foreign companies, and it ultimately did for us as well, though in a field that had little to do with those of Geotek's original holdings.

One of my first decisions at Geotek was to sell Apollo Lasers. Having shared offices with the company for a couple of years, I knew it had no future, mainly because it had not invested in technology for years. It was still showing decent revenue, however, which made it potentially attractive to other laser manufacturers looking to expand. As it happened, we were able to sell Apollo much more quickly than I had hoped. The buyer, a Florida-based competitor, paid Geotek $2M in cash. The only real downside to the deal was that it meant we had to find new office space.

There was little reason to stay in California once Apollo was no longer a part of Geotek, particularly since I had never understood why Dick Samuel chose to move Patlex out West in the first place. I decided on Philadelphia as Geotek's new home, largely because it was where I was most comfortable and well connected to the business community. It was easy for Geotek to move, as it had few employees in North America other than myself.

A few months after the move, the investigation of Geotek's activities by the Commerce Department in L.A. was finally completed. During the ensuing settlement talks, I learned that the investigation had been instigated by the discovery of a single unauthorized sale by Apollo Lasers to a Chinese customer. The sale had taken place in the early 1980s, well before either Patlex or Geotek had become associated with Apollo.

All the 18-month inquiry had been able to show was that this violation was probably the only one ever committed by either Apollo Laser or by any other Geotek company.

Geotek settled with the Commerce Department for a $21,000 fine, without admitting to any guilt. It was by all accounts a major victory. The fine amounted to less than 2% of the combined legal expenses of over $1M that Patlex and Geotek incurred during the investigation. It was not just because of the legal expenses, however, that the settlement came as a relief to me. Hagar and I had both recently applied for American citizenships. The investigation's closure meant that our approval was no longer at risk.

⁓

From 1989-1991, Geotek purchased two small companies in the U.S. to complement Oram and Reshef in Israel. The first of these was a factory in Connecticut, called TAC, which made custom-built power supplies. The strategy behind the acquisition was to combine TAC's operations with those of Oram in order to offer a more complete line of power-related products. It would be a major challenge, I knew, so I asked my father, who had done so well with Oram before, to head the new company. He agreed, coming to the U.S. shortly after we completed the acquisition and working out of TAC's offices in Connecticut.

Geotek's second purchase was of a small Yonkers, New York, defense company called Jericho, which specialized in the design and manufacture of mechanical fuzes, and sold only to the U.S. Department Of Defense. As with our previous acquisition, this one was also meant to complement an existing Geotek company, in this case, Reshef. Yoram Oron, Reshef's CEO came to the U.S. to supervise the combined company. It was our hope that having an American subsidiary would help Reshef break into the U.S defense market, which was notoriously unfriendly to foreign companies.

Aside from Yoram Oron and my father, there was one other person I invited to come to the U.S. and join Geotek. Yoram Bibring was a friend of mine, and he was a bright and resourceful public accountant. He had never before been a CFO, but I knew he would be up to the job. He was someone I could trust completely, and he proved himself over and over again, quickly becoming my closest advisor at Geotek.

In early 1991, I began to realize that Geotek needed to raise money as quickly as possible. The combination of a recession and the end of the Cold War, which had caused defense budgets worldwide to shrink, had hurt us a great deal, particularly since Reshef was our biggest company. Unfortunately, the financial markets were extremely tight in 1991, and the possibility of obtaining traditional financing for a small and risky company such as Geotek was all but nil. I decided, therefore, to turn to less conventional sources of capital, as I had done years before when no other options had been available to me.

The first investment obtained was from Sam Olly, a semi-retired entrepreneur, who agreed to lend Geotek $300K. The loan was guaranteed by some of Oram's property in Israel, and involved a significant number of stock options as an incentive. It was a tiny amount of money, but it gave Geotek enough breathing room to survive until a second, more rewarding, financing deal was signed a few months later. (Sam Olly exercised his options and sold his stocks at a profit of over a million dollars a couple of years later. It was a classic example of a "high risk-high return" investment.)

In one of my attempts to find an investor for Geotek, I arranged a meeting with Yoram Rosenfeld, the son of a former

Israeli media magnate (his father, Shalom Rosenfeld, had been the publisher of Maariv, one of Israel's biggest daily papers, for many years). Yoram ran a small, rather boring, private equity fund called USI, which was based in New York City. USI focused mainly on investments that had some Israeli connection, but it was not bound to this strategy, and it did have at least one major asset that was an exception to the rule. What it did not have was an ability to provide its investors with any liquidity, or at least some viable exit strategy. Given the recession both in Israel and the U.S., it was hardly surprising, therefore, that Yoram was coming under increasing amounts of pressure from his investors. When I came to him looking for an investment, he immediately saw in Geotek a potential solution to USI's liquidity problem. Instead of a capital investment, he suggested a different type of transaction - a merger. Geotek would issue publicly tradable stock to USI's investors, and, in exchange, would become the owner of USI's various diversified assets. Whatever money it generated from these could then be invested however it deemed appropriate, including in its own subsidiaries.

The negotiations with USI took several months to complete. The due diligence process was complicated by the fact that USI's holdings were disparate and showed little attempt at specialization. Of the lot, there were only two that I found at all interesting, but I did believe we would be able to sell off most of the other ones, even if only for small amounts of money. In a sense, the over-diversified nature of USI was almost an advantage for us, since it spread the risk among several fields. The reason USI had been unsuccessful, its unfocused approach to investing, was the same one that made it possible for me to sell off its various companies in a relatively short period of time. In a "Garage Sale" situation, it was good to have variety.

One of the reasons USI, and subsequently Geotek, had so many different assets was that it owned 33% of Yisum, a publicly-traded Israeli corporation that was itself a holding company. In addition to its stocks in Yisum, USI had voting agreements with some of the other shareholders, which gave it full control of the company. Yisum was over-diversified and, for the most part, non-synergetic. It owned companies in fields as unrelated as staffing, medical diagnostics, optics, and tropical fish cultivation. One of the only Yisum companies of any real value to Geotek was Aryt, a developer of specialty lenses for weapons systems, of which Yisum owned 50%. Aside from the fact that its product was genuinely promising, I believed Aryt to be a strong match for Geotek because our biggest strengths were in the same field, namely, defense. To capitalize on that, however, a major reorganization of both Aryt and Geotek's defense division would have to take place.

At the time of our merger with USI, Aryt had $10M in cash reserves and $10M in annual revenue. Its controlling shareholder, Yisum, had a nearly mature $10M debt, which stemmed from a loan it had taken years before in order to acquire its shares in Aryt. If Aryt could somehow merge with Geotek, however, much of the debt would effectively disappear, or rather, turn into equity, since the debtor and creditor would become one and the same, and the excess cash would be used to pay back the bank loan. In order to achieve this result, a complicated arrangement involving Geotek, Aryt and Yisum was engineered by Yoram Rosenfeld, Yoram Bibring and myself. In exchange for Aryt acquiring $10M worth of Geotek stock, Geotek transferred to it ownership of Reshef and Jericho. We then used roughly half of that money to pay our share of Yisum's debt, which left us with approximately $5M in cash. Aryt, meanwhile, became a much larger company,

with significantly expanded product lines and Yoram Oron as
its new CEO.

～～～～

While much of the motivation for restructuring Aryt and
Reshef was financial, it was also a product of a strategic shift
that Geotek was undergoing. I had begun to realize that my
initial strategy for the company, to focus on expanding our
defense and power divisions in the U.S., was not a realistic one
in the long term. There were two main reasons for this: firstly,
it had become clear to me that the defense sector would not
experience the kind of growth it had during the Reagan era
for some time; secondly, I had begun to understand that, even
if our numbers improved dramatically, the financial markets
would continue to penalize Geotek for its lack of focus.

Before Geotek's companies were spun-off from Patlex,
they never had to contend with the full ramifications of being
owned by the public, as they were never the focus of investors' attention. The laser patents were. They were what gave
Patlex its vision, and made the markets take notice. Because
the patents were "sexy" and generated excitement, investors
were willing to forgive Patlex its mistakes and support it
through years of financial losses and legal defeats. Geotek, I
realized, was exactly the opposite kind of company. Its vision
was simply not compelling enough. No-one was going to get
excited about Oram or Reshef landing a small contract, or
improving operating profits by ten or twenty percent. If
Geotek was to have any chance at prospering, rather than just
surviving, it had to present the financial markets with original
ideas. It had to present them with financial reports that included not just figures but plans for doing something *original*,
something that would give it an edge.

With this in mind, I decided to shift Geotek's focus to one of the few non-Israeli assets we acquired in the merger with USI, a stake in Bogen Communications. Bogen was a company that had been making commercial audio, amplification, and low-end communication equipment since 1932. It was well known in its field and had a large customer base of schools, factories and government institutions. It was also being mismanaged horribly and, as a result, was showing huge losses. In 1991, for example, it had lost $4M on revenue of $17M.

USI owned only about 20% of Bogen's shares, but it had lent the company $4M, money which Bogen showed no sign of being able to repay. Despite its losses Bogen was fundamentally a sound company with a valuable brand name. Many of its customers had been buying equipment from it for decades. While its technology was old, it had a position of respect in its market. Surely, with all it had going for it, it could be doing better than it was. The way I saw it, Bogen was Geotek's chance to get out of the stagnating defense and power fields and make a fresh start as a communications company, without having to build a new brand from scratch.

Bogen was effectively controlled by three major shareholders, who held positions of influence in both the company's management and its board of directors. Though the three were opposed to a takeover of Bogen by Geotek, they were unable to offer any alternative ways of paying their debt to use, and had no choice but to acquiesce to our demands. Thus, a few months after our merger with USI, I signed one more acquisition agreement, making Bogen a subsidiary of Geotek. What we would do with it, exactly, was something I still needed to figure out.

CHAPTER FOUR

DISCOVERING WIRELESS

In the fall of 1991, I was invited by an acquaintance of mine, Mark Solomon, to a half-philanthropic investment trip to Israel. The trip was being organized by Mark's firm, CMS, which was primarily in the insurance business. Its stated goal was to help Israel with its looming unemployment crisis, which was prompted by the enormous Jewish immigration from the soon to be dissolved Soviet Union. Since the immigrants were comprised in large part of well educated professionals, many with advanced degrees in scientific fields, it was deemed essential by both the Israeli government and Jewish philanthropic groups that employment opportunities created in Israel be geared towards a highly sophisticated workforce. The goal of our trip, therefore, was not merely to promote foreign investment, but to promote it in fields that would supply jobs that were highly productive and well paid.

Overall, the trip was interesting, but it was hardly a great success. We visited many places and got plenty of attention but nothing was done on a practical level. One of our visits was to a government-owned agency called Rafael, a highly secretive developer/manufacturer of advanced defense technologies, many of them exclusively designed for use by the

IDF. Rafael is located north of Haifa, the city where I grew up, and it had always held a certain mystique for me. As a child, I used to pass by its razor fences with my friends on the way to the beach town of Akko. I never knew what exactly they did inside the compound, and any references to Rafael in the media were inevitably so vague that they raised more questions than they answered.

We were treated well on our visit to Rafael, though the day scheduled for us had not been planned as thoroughly as I had become accustomed to in similar events in the U.S. Nevertheless, we met with several high-ranking officials in the organization, the most pertinent of which was Reuven Krupick, head of RDC - the Rafael Development Corporation. RDC was a joint venture of Rafael and Discount Investment Corporation, also known as IDB, a major Israeli investment group. Its purpose was to promote development of civilian applications for Rafael technologies. RDC had become increasingly important to Rafael by the early 1990s, as the defense industry in Israel was facing cuts in support from the government, and Rafael found itself in urgent need of additional sources of revenue.

One of the technologies Krupick highlighted in his presentation to us was Rafael's missile communication systems. These systems, he told us, utilized a proprietary method developed by Rafael to overcome radio frequency (RF) jamming, a commonly used technique for thwarting guided missiles that require constant contact with their weapons systems to operate effectively.

While I was impressed with the technologies Rafael presented to us, I did not come away from the meetings that day with any particular sense that Geotek should pursue a partnership with Rafael. Our focus was rapidly shifting from our defense division to Bogen, and Rafael was in many ways a typical defense contractor. I did inquire about its technologies in the audio field, but none of them appeared applicable to any product Bogen might want to offer.

Coming back to America, I remember thinking that the best aspect of the trip had been meeting Winston (Win) Churchill, the founder of CIP Capital, a venture capital fund. Win's background was in corporate law and mergers and ac-quisitions, and he had an enormous amount of experience and knowledge in all aspects of financing, particularly in the context of technology companies. Throughout the trip, Win and I had had many chances to talk, and we had resolved to meet again in the near future. Though I had not yet men-tioned it to him, I was already considering asking Win to in-vest in Geotek, and possibly even join its board of Directors.

The months following my return from the trip to Israel were extremely busy ones. Geotek had embarked on a major revi-talization campaign at Bogen, and most of my time was de-voted to that effort. It was a delicate operation in the way that the turnaround of a struggling company often is. There was an obvious need to replace many of Bogen's senior officers. At the same time, Bogen's greatest strength was its reputation as a stable, reliable vendor in an industry that valued these qualities a great deal. It was crucial, therefore, that the changes Geotek made at the sixty-five year old company would not be seen as disrespectful of its history and heritage.

In early 1992, Geotek moved from Philadelphia to Bogen's building in Ramsey, NJ. While the move was financially ben-eficial, it was also intended to be seen as a sign of our com-mitment to Bogen. Much of the battle, at least in the beginning, was just to energize the company: to spruce up its product line (even if major technological changes were not strictly necessary), to galvanize the sales force and supporting staff, and to bring marketing strategy into the 1990s. The last of these was particularly important, since one of the keys to improving sales was to impress upon existing customers, many of whom were using systems that were quite old, that Bogen's products were evolving.

In the long term, I knew that simply improving Bogen's performance would not solve Geotek's fundamental strategic problem of operating in low-tech markets of relatively little growth potential. The first step, however, was to gradually exit the defense field and reduce our reliance on shrinking government budgets and the politically influenced bureaucracies that controlled them. I had planned to begin looking for avenues of expansion for Bogen as soon as its losses subsided. Before Geotek had a chance to pursue this path, however, a much more exciting opportunity came along.

In late 1991, I received a lunch invitation from Irvin Gross, a businessman from Philadelphia whom I had met a couple of months earlier at the CMS-sponsored investment trip to Israel. Irvin had been one of the founders of International Mobile Machines (IMM), a wireless technology company that had gotten a great deal of attention in the 1980s (and later evolved into InterDigital Communications). IMM had been the foremost developer of the Time Division Multiple Access (TDMA) cellular standard, which was eventually adopted in nearly every country of the world (GSM, the standard adopted by the European Community and, subsequently, by many other countries was based on TDMA). IMM's great mistake had been focusing its energy on the field of fixed wireless, instead of cellular telephony. With fixed wireless networks, phones are limited in their location to one cell. They are wireless, but completely non-portable. IMM had envisioned the technology as a solution for third world countries looking to expand their primary phone systems while saving on the upstart costs of putting up telephone cables. The idea never gained much momentum, however, and by the time IMM realized this, it was too late for it to become a major player in the cellular field (such as its West Coast counterpart, Qualcomm). As for Irvin, he had since moved on to other ventures, including the company he was heading when we first met, which was developing some sort of revolutionary cooling technology. Our contact in Israel had been pretty limited, and I had no idea why he asked to see me, but I was curious, so I arranged to meet him at a restaurant near his office.

Over lunch, Irvin told me that, since returning from Israel, he had been devoting much of his time to trying to license the wireless communication technology Rafael had presented to us. This technology, he believed, had enormous potential for a variety of military and civilian wireless applications. It was what made Rafael's guided missile systems virtually immune to jamming, or interference. If he could license the technology, and perhaps make a few small modifications to it, Irvin thought there was a good chance the Pentagon would be interested in buying it from him, at a significant profit. Unfortunately, his negotiations with Rafael had hit an impasse. That was why he had contacted me. He needed a partner.

Irvin's decision to seek me out, rather than any number of better-financed investors, was surprising, but not without logic. Geotek did, after all, have a great deal of experience in dealing with both the Israeli and American defense establishments.

Furthermore, I was an Israeli, and though Rafael and RDC were eager for foreign investment, that did not mean familiarity with the local business and social culture had no advantages. For all his expertise and technical know-how, the executives at Rafael simply found Irvin strange. They were, for the most part, people who had spent much of their career in the Israeli Military, an establishment in which social niceties are rare even by Israel's notoriously non-formal standards. As I was soon to find out, one of the biggest reasons for the breakdown in the negotiations had been the fact that Reuven Krupick, the head of RDC, and others at Rafael, simply did not trust Irvin. They found the way he expressed himself highly suspect, and were frustrated by the fact that he could not demonstrate to them that he or his company were capable of delivering on all the promises he was making.

Though Irvin's proposal was intriguing, I told him right away that Geotek was trying to reduce its reliance on the defense market, and therefore could not consider making an investment predicated merely on possible interest by the Pentagon. It was at this point in our conversation that Irvin mentioned a more ambitious possibility. Throughout the U.S., he said, it was possible to buy certain cellular frequencies very cheaply. The FCC had long ago designated these small parts of the spectrum for use by Specialized Mobile Radio, or SMR. Specialized Mobile Radio systems were those commonly used by fleets for traditional push-to-talk wireless communication. Though the SMR frequencies were in the same part of the spectrum as cellular frequencies, they were considered much less valuable because they were non-continuous, which made them unsuitable for large-capacity cellular networks. The technology developed by Rafael, however, was uniquely suited for deployment in these types of non-continuous spectrums. In other words, Irvin said, it could be used as the core technology for wireless networks that relied on very inexpensive electromagnetic real estate.

As Irvin and I parted ways, after a meeting that had lasted far longer than I had expected, my head was spinning with ideas. It seemed absurdly ambitious, of course, but somehow Irvin made his proposal sound downright achievable. Although I left the meeting the way I did countless others, with nothing but a promise to look into the matters raised, I was unusually excited this time. It was a long shot, I realized, but nevertheless I was anxious to start looking into a field about which I knew next to nothing, other than the fact that it was sure to explode in the coming decade.

～～･～～

In the weeks that followed my meeting with Irvin, I spent much of my time speaking to anyone I could think of, either from the U.S. or Israel, who was knowledgeable about the business or technological aspects of the wireless industry. Irvin, meanwhile, was still unsure whether he was willing to give up on his original plan of licensing Rafael's technology for military use. After a few additional meetings, however, both Irvin and I were ready to form a new venture and start the process of negotiating with RDC as partners. We agreed on a 60/40 split in ownership, with Geotek, the controlling shareholder, providing initial funding of $1M. We named the new venture Power Spectrum Inc., or PSI, and I became its CEO.

Since Irvin had long since lost any good will there had been towards him by RDC and Rafael, I became the main negotiator for PSI. Overall, RDC and Rafael were quite reasonable in their demands, but somewhat dishonest, or at least misleading, in the way they presented their technology. They did not lie to us, exactly, but they did imply that adapting their communication technology to support the required cellular features, particularly voice transmission, would be far easier than it eventually proved. It was a classic example of the importance of due diligence, and though at the time I believed that we were being careful, I later realized that we should have asked many more questions. To dissuade our concerns regarding the scope of the project necessary to adapt the Rafael technology to our needs, Reuven Baron, a senior Rafael officer, came to one of the negotiation meetings carrying three large electronics boards. These boards, he indicated, showed the technology's fully developed state. It was an exercise in theatrics, and we should not have allowed it to have an impact on our decision-making.

One of the reasons I felt so confident about the emerging deal was the positive results of an evaluation of Rafael's technology performed by George Calhoun, an industry veteran I had hired at Irvin's suggestion. George was enormously knowledgeable about cellular technology, so when he urged me to sign a deal with RDC before some other company beat us to it, I took his advice very seriously. Ultimately, his analysis had been solid, in that it primarily addressed the question of whether Rafael's technology could be adapted to our needs, not how much it would cost (both in terms of money and time) to do so. The framing of questions when performing due diligence is critical, and ours was certainly flawed.

The contract we signed with RDC, in June of 1992, was remarkably short for a document that became the cornerstone of a six-year relationship that brought over $100 million worth of business to Rafael. PSI agreed to invest an initial sum of $4M in the wireless venture. Its initial and most critical task, it was agreed, would be to provide Rafael with a feature specifications document detailing the requirements of the system it envisioned. In exchange for PSI's commitment, it was given an irrevocable license for the terrestrial commercial rights to Rafael's communication technology, known as frequency hopping. Additionally, both sides agreed that Rafael would act as a sub-contractor to PSI, under terms that would be negotiated periodically. A special group in Rafael's electronics division was to be created for this purpose. Lastly, once development was completed, Rafael and PSI would also become OEM partners, with PSI purchasing from Rafael some of the critical pieces of hardware required to build cellular base stations. One of the reasons that many details were left to be negotiated in the future was that, at the time, we were still unsure whether PSI's main focus would be on bringing its technology to the market directly, by creating a network, or indirectly, by selling equipment to service providers. Though Irv Gross and I had discussed the idea of acquiring spectrum licenses for a new network, the issue was still far from being decided when we signed our initial contract with RDC.

───•───

Soon after the agreement with Rafael was signed, we created an Israeli subsidiary for PSI, called Power Spectrum Technology LTD, or PST, to work directly with Rafael on technology development. PST was given use of a building inside Rafael's compound, and its initial staff came entirely from Rafael. Some of these employees were ones that had been looking to leave anyway, while others were simply taking a sabbatical. In both cases, Rafael was happy to recommend them to PST, as that way they could continue to contribute to the organization indirectly. Throughout the years, many of PST's employees came to us via the sabbatical program, which proved to be a potent but dangerous resource, as PST's requests to keep sabbatical employees longer than the prescribed year was a constant source of tension in its relationship with Rafael.

One of the first major decisions PSI had to make with regard to PST was the selection of its CEO. Since PST would be subcontracting much of the actual development to Rafael, it was crucial that its CEO be someone who was extremely familiar with the organization and knew how to get results from it. For all the brilliance of its engineers, Rafael was ultimately a typical government-owned agency in terms of its office politics and excessive bureaucracy. I was convinced, therefore, that only someone who had worked within the system would have the necessary skills and know-how to effectively manage Rafael's work on our project from the outside. As a result, I limited the search for CEO to candidates presented by Rafael. Eventually, I decided on a long-time Rafael employee by the name of David Tamir, whose position in 1992 was as Rafael's representative in the United States, working from Washington, D.C. It was a decision I have since looked back on with mixed feelings. While David did prove to be the kind of strong, demanding manager that PST needed, he lacked the diplomatic skill necessary to keep tensions from exploding. As eager as he was to fight for the resources PST had to have, he was equally apt to get into altercations for small matters that could have been resolved much more easily had he shown some finesse and willingness to compromise. Many people told me back then, and in the years since, that I would have been better off hiring a CEO from the private sector. In retrospect, however, I still believe that I made the right decision. Either way, it was a one of enormous significance for Geotek. For the following three years, until the development of the core technology was completed, Geotek's fate was closely linked to David's ability to manage, under far from optimal conditions, the huge tasks with which he was charged.

To counteract David's shortcomings, I asked my uncle, Shalom Eitan, who had been a Vice President of an Israeli telephony company called Tadiran, to become PST's Chairman of the Board. Shalom was my late father's brother, and I had always had a lot of respect for his capabilities and strong personality. Though the position did not involve direct authority over day-to-day operations, Shalom became very active at PST and proved himself enormously valuable on countless occasions, particularly when it came to smoothing things over with Rafael and keeping David and his management team "honest" and on target. His presence at PST gave me much piece of mind, since I trusted his judgment and knew that he would keep me accurately informed even if others preferred not to do so. It was extremely important to me to have someone at PST whom I could trust to look out for the larger interests of PSI.

Though the focus of Geotek's wireless division was in Israel, several key people joined the company in the U.S. as well. One of the earliest of these was George Calhoun, whom I had first hired as a consultant during the negotiations with RDC. George had been one of the original founders of IMM, and I was rather surprised when he agreed, at that stage of his career, to become President of Geotek's still tiny wireless division. Nevertheless, he fit in extremely well at Geotek, and quickly became one of the its most influential executives. He was also the only Geotek officer, other than myself, who was invited to join the Board of Directors. Along with Yoram Bibring, Geotek's CFO, George became one of my closest advisors, and remained so until nearly the end of my tenure at the company. For all his strengths, however, he was not a strong operations man, and his influence at Geotek was mostly the result of the confidence that I, and some of our biggest investors, placed in him.

The second major figure to join Geotek after our move into wireless, in 1992, was Eyal Kaplan, a talented consultant I hired as our VP of Marketing. Eyal contributed greatly to Geotek's initial positioning as a provider of value-added services, particularly when it came to highlighting the advantages of combining SMR-type services with advanced data functionality. He was also, however, an exceedingly difficult person to work with, quick to dismiss views that contradicted his own, and, as a result, grew increasingly marginalized as Geotek expanded. Nevertheless, by virtue of the work he did early on, along with George Calhoun and a few others who joined Geotek in its early days, Eyal played an important and positive role in shaping the company's long-term direction.

All of us were very enthusiastic about the road ahead, but none of us had any real understanding of the length and difficulty of the journey we had embarked upon. The good news was that our timing was right, as the wireless field was just beginning to get an enormous amount of attention from the financial markets, and the issue of migration from analog to digital technologies was on everyone's mind. We had limited resources and expertise, however, and a plan that would likely require us to become both a technology innovator and an operator of a logistically complex, not to mention costly, commercial wireless network.

CHAPTER FIVE

GEOTEK'S TECHNOLOGY AND VISION

The early nineties were a time of great anticipation, as well as uncertainty, in the cellular field. After years of relatively slow technological and commercial growth, it was clear to nearly all who followed the industry that it was headed in a direction of major changes, driven by increases in both the number of subscribers and the average amount of air-minutes used by each one. Two revolutionary digital protocols held out promise for transforming wireless networks worldwide, increasing capacity several times over and enabling all sorts of new features. Though both technologies were still years away from wide-scale deployment, industry analysts were already spending a good deal of their time trying to predict whether TDMA (Time Division Multiple Access) or CDMA (Code Division Multiple Access) would emerge as the dominant standard. Of the two technologies, TDMA was the more mature one. The choice of GSM, which was based on it, as the European standard, was the first major victory in the battle between the two competing digital technologies.

Adopting either TDMA or CDMA, it was clear, would require enormous investments by dozens of cellular service providers scattered throughout America. Already, what had started out as an industry comprised of independent regional companies had gone through major consolidation. McCaw Cellular, for example, had acquired so many spectrums and regional providers throughout the 1980s that it had become a de-facto national provider (it became the foundation for AT&T Wireless after AT&T acquired it for $11.5B in 1994). Even companies that remained independent banded into a large partnership, called Cellular One, in order to be able to offer their customers national roaming capabilities. In short, the cellular industry was moving in a direction very different than the one envisioned by the FCC when it had first given away cellular spectrums *by lottery* in the 1970s and 1980s (In the mid 1990s, it auctioned similar licenses for billions of dollars).

The two-way radio, or commercial wireless, field was also heading for major changes. Motorola, the industry's most influential provider of technology, and biggest owner of frequencies, was developing a digital communications platform called MIRS, or Motorola Integrated Radio System. MIRS, which was later given the more neutral-sounding name iDEN (Integrated Dispatch Enhanced Network), was based on TDMA, but geared and optimized for commercial wireless systems. Although it did not become widely available until the mid 1990s, the mere fact that Motorola had decided to invest in developing iDEN sent a powerful signal to the industry that the days of simple analog Specialized Mobile Radio, or SMR, were numbered.

One other major shift was beginning to take place in the commercial wireless world. In January of 1992, several months before Geotek partnered with Rafael, a two-way radio service provider called Fleet Call filed for a NASDAQ IPO. Since being founded in 1987 by Morgan O'Brien, a former FCC staffer, Fleet Call had been quietly buying up frequencies and private radio operators throughout the U.S. It had also developed a close relationship with Motorola, not only because it was a major provider of analog equipment, but also in anticipation of the arrival of MIRS, which would support a combined push-to-talk and cellular service. Fleet Call's IPO gave it the money to intensify its M&A campaign, which consisted mostly of acquiring "mom and pop" SMR operations, and the company soon became the industry leader, changing its name to Nextel Communications.

One of the most crucial decisions Geotek and PSI had to make was what type of business model we would adopt for the venture, what, exactly, we would *sell*. We knew we would develop an advanced cellular system based on Rafael's frequency hopping technology. We also knew that that system would be designed to support private radio applications, both because Irvin Gross and I believed commercial wireless would become more lucrative (and less competitive) than cellular, and because frequency hopping was ideally suited for the discontinuous spectrums typically allocated for SMR. What was not so obvious, however, was how PSI would bring its technology to the market, what it would actually *do* once development had ended. For a product as monumental in scope as an entirely new cellular technology, there were only two options PSI could pursue: it could try to license its technology to service providers, and sell them equipment and support, or it could become a service provider itself, selling directly to end-users. If it chose the former option, it would have to compete with the likes of Motorola, Qualcomm and Nokia; if it chose the latter, its competitors would be the baby Bells, McCaw Cellular and Fleet Call, among others.

The biggest advantage to becoming a pure technology company was that it would have allowed PSI to concentrate on development without having to worry about setting up the vast physical and organization infrastructure necessary to support a cellular network. No wireless company had ever succeeded in being both a technology developer and a major cellular service provider. Even Motorola, the field's 800 lbs Gorilla, which had once owned cellular networks all over the world, had, by the early 1990s, scaled down much of its international service operations. In the U.S., where it owned a significant percentage of the SMR spectrum, it did own some SMR networks as well, but it also leased many of its frequencies to other providers, which typically bought equipment from it too. The reason Motorola never tried to become a major cellular provider in the U.S. was that selling equipment was its prime objective, and it did not want to compete with its own customers. As many technology companies have discovered over the years, providing service directly to end-users requires innovation of a very different type than the one needed to create a physical product. (While Thomas Edison may have invented the kinetoscope, his film studio could not sustain its early success once the initial novelty of moving images had worn off.)

The barriers to PSI entering the cellular market as a pure technology provider, however, would have been vast. The difficulty was not just in the fact that we would have had to compete with bigger and more established competitors, it was also in the very nature of the product we would be trying to sell. It is difficult enough to convince a major cellular provider to commit to even a handset made by an upstart company; in our case, the commitment required would have been much greater. A provider interested in frequency hopping technology would have had to rely on PSI for nearly every piece of cellular equipment it used. If PSI were to fold, its entire infra-structure would become endangered, as technical support and spare parts would become a thing of the past. Few network operators were likely to accept that risk. In addition, even though the FCC did not impose any specific standards on the industry, various de-facto standards had been created over the years by operators and equipment providers, and using them made the challenges of running a network far more manageable.

In terms of potential upside, it was clear to me that the service provider option was the more attractive one. At the end of the day, nearly every technology product that can be sold in a box eventually becomes a commodity. No one is willing to pay a premium very long for a cellular sub-station hidden in a large closet somewhere. A service provider, how-ever, can build a brand, even in the cutthroat wireless indus-try. It can offer features, customization and convenience for which users are happy to pay, particularly the business users two-way radio applications can attract. Nextel, which became Geotek's biggest competitor, is an example of this earnings potential – though it has emerged as the smallest network in terms of total users, it has by far the highest revenue per sub-scriber. It also has the industry's second lowest churn rate, meaning it can keep its marketing costs far lower than those of companies such as Cingular or T-Mobile, which are con-stantly fighting to replace lost customers. By capitalizing on our unique frequency hopping technology, I saw a way to build a business with very low marginal costs and recurring revenue from wireless users.

With these considerations in mind, we chose to pursue a vision of PSI as a service, rather than technology, provider. The decision meant that it would have to become an enor-mously complex company. Nevertheless, PSI was still a technology company, and we all saw it as such. For the time being, no one seemed to mind this duality of purpose. Eventually, however, the tension between the two competing visions of the company would take its toll.

I have looked back at our critical decision to become a service provider many times over the years, and am as convinced today as I was in 1992 that it was the right one. It was a difficult but brave choice, and it demonstrated our willingness to "dream big" and wake up every morning with the energy and drive to make our vision happen. I now realize, however, that keeping the service and the technology divisions under one roof was a mistake. As a young company with limited resources and experience, we simply did not have the ability to properly deal with the complexity of these two very different organizations rolled into one. Had I realized early on how complicated it would be to build a service providing organization, I suspect I would have looked for ways to limit the burdens we faced, and thus increase our chances of succeeding.

The technology PSI licensed from Rafael was known as *frequency hopping*. It was developed to allow for very secure and robust wireless communication channels, such as the ones used to combat the problem of jamming in missile-guidance applications. A guided missile, by its very nature, must be able to communicate reliably with its ground command and control station. The most common approach to combating a guided missile, therefore, is to jam the communication channel it uses to "talk" to its weapons system. In the typical analog model of wireless communication, the task is almost trivial. All an anti-missile system needs to do is scan the radio spectrum, detect which frequency is being used by the missile, and transmit something, anything, in that frequency. Rafael's approach to solving this problem was to change the nature of the communication channel. In a frequency hopping system, the two communicating parties switch transmission frequencies simultaneously, at a rate of several hundred switches per second, based on a predetermined *hopping sequence*. The "channel" becomes an amalgam of frequencies, analogous to water constantly adjusting course between a series of rapidly opening and closing pipes.

Aside from the fact that it could be used relatively easily over discontinuous spectrums, frequency hopping was well suited to cellular and commercial wireless systems for another crucial reason - it provided a dramatic advantage in service quality over fixed-frequency systems (such as TDMA and GSM). This was the result of the fact that "bad" frequencies could effect communication only during the miniscule spans of time when a hopping channel happened to use them. The overall effect of interference was greatly diminished in frequency hopping systems by the fact that it was spread out equally among so many channels. Instead of one user experiencing a 50% loss of call quality, for example, a hundred users might encounter a virtually unnoticeable .5% loss.

For all its potential, however, frequency hopping was not a *cellular* technology. It was a core RF communications technology that had to be adapted to complicated real-world applications. One of the first decisions we had to make was which name to give the final "application" technology. Taking a cue from the industry's standard naming scheme, we settled on Frequency Hopping Multiple Access, or FHMA (a derivative, like TDMA and CDMA, of Frequency Division Multiple Access (FDMA) – the name of the first – analog – generation of cellular technology).

In broad terms, it was the "MA" part of FHMA that PST, with the help of Rafael, needed to develop. Multiple access meant simply that the system had to support voice and data communication between base stations and multiple subscriber units, typically in the form of vehicle-based terminals. In that simple term, however, lay the crux of the challenge PST faced – it had to turn a technology built to communicate with a small number of missiles for just a few minutes at a time into one capable of sustaining a constantly operating network of thousands of mobile phones talking to one another and accessing the public switched telephone network (PSTN).

FHMA was designed from the beginning as a Hybrid of state of the art technologies, the most important of which was frequency hopping. It contained elements of the two main digital cellular protocols, TDMA and CDMA, which had been fighting for dominance of the wireless industry since the early 1990s. Like TDMA, FHMA utilized a time division algorithm, which worked by organizing digital communication into time slots, with three compressed packets of data in each one. This technology allowed each FHMA channel to be used by three callers at a time. Unlike TDMA, however, FHMA used additional techniques to increase capacity too.

FHMA's similarity to CDMA came from the fact that both utilized multiple frequencies for each transmission (CDMA, like FHMA, originated from technology developed to avoid jamming in military applications). In a CDMA system, a subscriber unit transmits to a wide spectrum of at least 1.25 MHz, or fifty times the size of a typical TDMA channel. It determines which frequency contains the data meant for it to "play" at any given time based on *headers* placed at the beginning of each transmitted packet. These headers contain identifiers unique to each phone on the network. Though both CDMA and FHMA phones were designed to listen to a broad spectrum of several MHz, FHMA subscriber units *transmitted* on much narrower 25 KHz channels. These channels, however, was not comprised of single frequencies but rapidly changing ones. If an FHMA transmission is modeled by water flowing through a series of opening and closing pipes, a CDMA transmission is analogous to a tiny stream emerging from a source (the phone or cellular base station) into a wide river. The brilliance of CDMA lies in the algorithms that reassemble the transmission at each end, essentially splitting the river back into countless streams that are exactly identical to the original ones.

One important element in the design of FHMA was *cell sectorization*. Since channels that utilized frequency hopping could sustain such a high level of interference at acceptable call quality, the technology was uniquely suited to support high capacity networks with excellent *frequency reuse ratios*. PST decided, therefore, to adopt a *sectorized macro-cellular* approach in the design of FHMA. One of the difficulties in this approach, which meant that cells would be quite large by industry standards, was in ensuring the cells would be able to support sufficient capacity. Typically, to add capacity, a provider must increase either the frequency count or the number of cells covering the region it serves. With FHMA, we attempted to minimize this limitation by breaking up cells into radial *sectors*, shaped like slices of pie. A sector in FHMA was designed to differ from a cell in one crucial way – its unique characteristic was a set of hopping sequences rather than a frequency spectrum. By assigning orthogonal sets of hopping sequences to each transmission, and adding error-correction codes to all calls, it was possible to minimize the interference encountered at sectors' fringes as a result of frequency collisions. Essentially, FHMA utilized frequency hopping as a sophisticated way of implementing a mild form of code division without explicit codes (and the vast complexities associated with them).

Taken together, FHMA's use of sectorization and time division made the system PSI proposed in 1992 as efficient, in terms of capacity, as any potential competing cellular system, including CDMA. In its ability to use discontinuous spectrums, however, FHMA was unmatched. No other technology allowed service providers to effectively utilize spectrums as small as 250 KHz to provide mobile communication services on a mass scale. Even today, this capability is virtually impossible to obtain at any economically viable cost.

—◡•◡—

For all its complexity, FHMA's core architecture was determined very quickly. It was mainly about creating a multi-channel, high capacity system (a well understood concept, which we certainly did not need to re-invent) utilizing the frequency hopping technology familiar to the Rafael team. Where PSI had much more difficulty was in adequately defining the specifics, in detailing the hundreds of critical requirements of the system PST was to develop and coming up with a realistic projection of the true complexity and scope of the development process. Rafael's engineers knew very little about commercial applications, such as voice communication. The challenge was for the developers to acquire these expertise quickly and then design a system that would be flexible and reliable enough for a commercial environment with many thousands of users.

The first major task PSI had to do was to write up a detailed system requirements document. While this document did not need to be very technical, it was essential that it addressed every operation a system user or administrator might want to perform. Determining requirements for a system as complex as a cellular network, let alone one based on such untried technology as FHMA, is an enormous job. It was a testament to our naivety that we believed we would be capable of completing it in just three months, with little outside help, while simultaneously working to raise at least $4M to finance development in Israel. My primary objective, at the time, was to see the development team start the actual development work. I underestimated the importance of detailed planning, and Geotek paid a heavy price for that later.

Back when I was in the infantry, one of the battalion commanders used to instruct us that if ever we came under fire, the most critical step, after finding cover, was to take as much time as necessary to plan ahead. Only once all possibilities had been examined, he told us, should we proceed - as swiftly as we could. In 1992, PSI did not take the time to review its options. I suspect that if it had, if I had pushed it in the right direction, Geotek would ultimately have saved both money and time.

For the most part, the problems with the requirements spec, which was finally completed in early 1993, were far from earth shattering. They resulted in development headaches and some cost overruns, but not much more. Taken together, however, the relatively small omissions and ambiguities that entered the requirements document had a greater toll than might have been expected, partly because it was easy to let them percolate through the development process. The problem was not that any one of those early mistake could not be rectified (they could), but that they resulted in a system that was not as "clean" as it should have been. Had PSI dedicated the resources to creating a more detailed spec, the completed system most likely would not have been all that different from the one that was actually developed. It would, however, have had fewer bugs, needed less "patches," and been far easier to maintain and troubleshoot. Furthermore, it would almost certainly have been completed closer to schedule, as PSI and PST would not have set such unreasonable timetables for themselves. In 1998, when things looked dire for us, I used to say that if we had had our present experience back in 1992, Geotek could have developed FHMA in half the time and at half the cost of the eventual development program.

One of PSI's smartest decisions had been to insist, from the very beginning, that the system we developed with Rafael be designed from the ground up to support data as well as voice communication. We even made sure that IP (Internet Protocol) was the protocol used for data encapsulation. The spec did not, however, go any deeper than that fundamentally technical level, and that was its biggest flaw. Most crucially, it did not detail what *kind* of data-related applications the FHMA system would support. This omission ended up costing Geotek more than any other, both in terms of cost overruns and in time-to-market.

Ultimately, our failure to deliver a spec that was sufficiently accurate and useful was a symptom of our lack of experience. For all the enthusiasm of everyone involved, the management team that ran Geotek and PSI in the first half of the 1990s was made up of relative novices, and we all had to learn as we went. None of us, least of all myself, suspected that the venture Geotek had embarked upon would require nearly the kind of resources that it eventually consumed, or that the complexity of developing our U.S. network, GeoNet, would be so great. Had PSI had the human resources to do the kind of thorough marketing requirements research that it should have, it is quite possible it would have decided to significantly limit the scope of its plans even before development began. Such a decision might have prevented Geotek's eventual downfall, though it could just as likely have prevented us from getting off the ground to begin with. In early 1993, a Rafael official predicted the PST project would cost $30M. The amount sounded staggering to me. Eventually, the technology development alone cost Geotek over $100M. The fact that we were naïve, that we lacked experience and were not so intimidated by "reality," did a great deal to help Geotek forward its ambitious plans.

CHAPTER SIX
GOING ALL IN

Aside from the specification of system requirements, the most immediate task Geotek faced in the second half of 1992 was raising funds to support PSI and PST. While the agreement with Rafael did not require PSI to write a check for its full $4M commitment right away, we did need to start funding PST's operations. Furthermore, it was clear that $4M could hardly sustain PST through the entire development cycle, though none of us could imagine what a tiny fraction of Geotek's full investment that initial sum would eventually be. Even under the rosiest estimates, however, there was no denying that we needed to raise some serious money, fast.

Fortunately, Geotek was already in an unusually strong financial position by the time the Rafael deal was completed. Early in 1992, as we began negotiations with RDC, I also started a dialog with a "boutique" investment banking firm called Laidlaw Capital Management. Laidlaw's main business was managing money for wealthy individuals, and, as a result, it was always in the market for opportunities it could offer its clients that were not readily available through standard channels. In the beginning, my discussions with Laidlaw focused mainly on the changes Geotek wanted to make at Bogen. As negotiations with RDC progressed, however, I started to present the prospect of a wireless venture as well, even though it was still far too speculative to make it the central theme of my pitch.

Whatever it was that ultimately attracted Laidlaw to Geotek, they agreed to promote it among their clients with a private placement stock offering. To make the offer more appealing, Laidlaw suggested that we use a financial instrument that bundled stocks and options. In return for buying Geotek stocks priced at around $1.35, a 10% discount from the share's market price, each investor also received a proportional number of options to buy additional stocks at $2.10. Though this arrangement would eventually dilute Geotek's stock even more, it allowed us to raise $5M at a time in which, due to the recession, the financial markets were still quite unreceptive to small, risky companies.

Little more than a year before the Laidlaw offering successfully closed, I had been struggling to secure a private $300K loan from Sam Olly in order to keep Geotek solvent. Now, with Geotek working to revitalize Bogen and start a brand new wireless business, our cash needs were many times greater. The $5M we had just raised, I could see, would support us for no more than a few months.

Shortly after returning to the U.S. from the signing of PSI's contract with RDC, I contacted an acquaintance of mine at Lehman Brothers to discuss Geotek's situation. We were too small to be of any real interest to his firm, so he referred me to Gary Fuhrman, a partner at the small, "white-shoe" firm of Arnhold and S. Bleichroeder. Though most of Arnhold and S. Bleichroeder's business was in managing portfolios for wealthy individuals, it also represented some substantial corporate clients, mostly of German origin, in their American

M&A activities. Despite our considerable differences in background and demeanor, Gary and I understood and respected one another from the start, and he became one of Geotek's most influential early supporters in the financial industry. Shortly after our first meeting, Gary agreed to sponsor the company's second private placement offering of 1992. Partly because of the improved prospects of Bogen, our share price had risen significantly by this point, to around $3, and Gary was able to convince his firm's clients to invest a total of $15M in Geotek. It was an enormous sum for us.

—◡•◡—

1993 was a year of great growth for Geotek. Once the system requirements specification had finally been completed, development at PST and Rafael began in earnest. I started spending much of my time shuttling from Haifa to Ramsey, NJ, an arduous travel schedule that would lighten only a couple years later, when the focus of Geotek's operations shifted back to the U.S. There were some who were critical of the fact that my involvement in R&D was so hands-on. I believed, however, that it was necessary because of David Tamir's inability to maintain a civil relationship with the Rafael brass, on which we were highly dependent. No one understood frequency hopping as well as a few select engineers at Rafael's electronics division, so it was critical that PSI and Geotek remain in the good graces of those who controlled their assignments. For the most part, we managed to get Rafael's brightest and most knowledgeable employees on our team, but it took constant negotiation. One of our biggest disappointments in this regard was that we were never able to convince Rafael to assign to the project a truly first-rate software expert. Rafael's strengths had always been in hardware, and it refused to view the PSI project from the same software-centric perspective that we did. Eventually, we had no choice but to hire someone from the outside to head PST's software development group.

In the first quarter of 1993, Geotek's board, which was headed by Win Churchill (whom I had invited to join in late 1992) grew increasingly optimistic about the prospects of the company's wireless venture. The cellular field was hotter than ever, and, after a rocky start, development in Israel on FHMA had finally begun. Equally as important, the relative ease with which we had managed to raise $20M in the 1992 convinced Geotek's directors, myself included, that the time was ripe to take a chance and "invest big." Bogen had also turned a corner, so when Speech Design, a German company that had developed an innovative speech-processing technology, came on the block, we negotiated a merger for the two companies. More importantly, Geotek's board also decided to try to buy out Irving Gross's 40% stake in PSI. The reasons for this were twofold: firstly, we believed that the value of PSI would grow immensely in the coming years, and, secondly, the relationship with Irvin had quickly soured during our short partnership. Though Irvin was a visionary, he was also temperamental, stubborn and difficult to work with. He seemed oblivious, sometimes, of immediate financial considerations, and was resentful of the fact that Geotek would not allow PSI to switch directions whenever he had a new idea. It was, in many ways, typical of the tensions that often arise in joint ventures between companies and individuals. Irvin simply could not relate to the needs of a publicly traded organization such as Geotek. Ultimately, however, he did realize that, as a minority shareholder who could not contribute to PSI financially, he would not be allowed to play the kind of dominant role in the venture that he would have liked. As a result, he agreed, in the spring of 1993, to sell Geotek his share of PSI in a stock deal. Once the buyout was completed, Geotek turned PST into a direct subsidiary and PSI ceased to exist. For Irvin, the sale of his stake in PSI proved to be very profitable. During the year that followed the transaction, he sold the Geotek shares he had received for an amount that was likely higher than $20M.

At about the same time that we ended our partnership with Irvin, we also dissolved our last connection to the Patlex period. As a result of the restructuring of Yissum (of which Geotek had gained control in 1991, through the merger with USI), Geotek still had a major stake in Aryt, which in turn was one of our biggest shareholders. As we had little interest in the defense field anymore, we decided that the time was right for the two companies to go their separate ways. Since each company's stake in the other was worth roughly the same amount, we agreed with Aryt on a simple stock swap deal. It was a well-timed anti-diluting transaction, from Geotek's perspective, since the value of the company's stock rose rapidly in the years that followed, a trend that benefited from the decrease in the number of tradable Geotek shares. Upon completion of this transaction, Geotek ceased to be a diverse holding company and became a communications company only. It was still not a focused company, however, since we did own the low-tech Bogen as well as PSI.

Although the bulk of Geotek's expansion continued to take place is Israel, through PST, our skeletal wireless team in the U.S. grew as well. One influential senior executive I hired was Dr. Oliver Hilsenrath, an electronics engineer Irvin Gross had recommended to me shortly before our partnership ended.

Oliver had once been an employee of Rafael, but by the time I hired him, as Geotek's Chief Technology Officer, he had been living in the U.S. for some time and was no longer affiliated with his former employer. His past experience with Rafael was certainly a plus for us, however, and his ideas and unique expertise contributed greatly to many aspects of the technology we developed. His influence at Geotek was especially high during his first couple of years with the company. Over time, however, he became somewhat marginalized. Partly this was the result of the shifting of resources and focus away from technological development, but a more crucial reason was that Oliver was so difficult to work with. He had little patience for colleagues who exhibited less intelligence than his own, and was incapable of seeing the big picture. He was brilliant when it came to analysis, but would often make unwise, or at least unrealistic, decisions based on his (correct) conclusions.

A less controversial figure that joined Geotek's core new management team during this period of rapid growth was George Polk, our Vice President for Business Development. George, who was an excellent "deal-maker," played an important early role in advancing two of Geotek's biggest strategic pursuits: acquiring spectrum licenses domestically and expanding internationally. In the latter category, we were presented with a major opportunity just a few short months after George joined Geotek.

In the fall of 1993, Gary Fuhrman told me about a struggling British commercial wireless provider that had recently been put on the block. The company, National Band Three (NB3), was a subsidiary of Vodafone, and though its performance in the early 1990s had been less than stellar, it had a customer base of about 30,000 subscribers, a very substantial number for the private radio industry at the time. Geotek had just recently purchased its first set of frequencies in the U.S., from a provider in Washington, DC, and it seemed as good a time as any to begin exploring international expansion possibilities too. Gary Fuhrman and I flew out to London, therefore, and, over a lunch of bad British sandwiches with Vodafone's CEO and CFO, agreed, in principal, to a cash purchase of NB3 at its book value of £10.5M, or over $20M. In retrospect, I have come to view this decision as overly ambitious, and, ultimately, unwise. As a small company still in the early stages of developing its product, we should have waited until we had established a foothold in the U.S. market before venturing internationally. Though NB3 proved to be a good investment from a financial point of view, Geotek spent resources on it that it would have been better off directing elsewhere.

A few weeks after our meeting with Vodafone, once Geotek's initial due diligence had found little reason not to go forward with the NB3 purchase, I met with Gary again to discuss our options for financing the deal. What Geotek needed, it was clear, was a substantial new investor. The reason was simple: we had become too big for private placement deals of the type that had sustained us in the past, while remaining too small to employee other types of financing schemes, such as issuing debt or doing a secondary public stock offering. What Geotek needed, in other words, was to raise money from "institutional" investors, ones that would buy into our vision and be able to support it in a substantial way.

At Gary's suggestion, I met with a friend of his, Gary Siegler, who headed the mid-sized hedge fund of Siegler Collery, whose total net asset value was in the low hundreds of millions of dollars. My pitch for Geotek and FHMA was pretty well practiced by this point, and after we had spent a

couple of hours talking, Gary Siegler agreed to study the possibility of a major investment further. Upon completing their
analysis a week later, Siegler Collery offered to invest $25M in
Geotek. The financial instrument they wanted to use however
- a preferred, convertible, variable-priced stock - was a somewhat uncommon one. A typical convertible stock can be redeemed (i.e. converted into a common share) at a fixed price
determined at the time of issuing. A variable-priced convertible, in contrast, is redeemed at a price based on the *common*
share's value *at the time of conversion*. In our case, Siegler Collery
requested a conversion price of 90% the cost of a common
share. Under this scheme, the potential upside, compared to
that of fixed-price convertible, was slightly limited, but the
risk was diminished tremendously. The only way Siegler Collery
could lose money with this kind of investment was if Geotek
went out of business or became otherwise illiquid. So long as
that did not happen, the investment was a sure thing, since
Siegler Collery could always "buy" common shares at a discount to their market price.

Surprisingly, the use of a variable-priced convertible stock
had a major potential benefit for Geotek as well. The higher
the price of our stock went, the less shares Siegler Collery
could redeem for its $25M investment. The flip side of this,
however, was that if our share price dropped, Siegler Collery
would be able to redeem their preferred instrument for more
common stocks. Since both Geotek's board and I believed
that the company would continue growing, however, we felt
comfortable about accepting this risk and agreeing to Siegler
Collery's terms.

The preferred variable-priced convertibles we issued in
late 1993 were eventually converted in only 1995, when our
share price was roughly twice as high as when the Siegler

Collery stocks were first issued. The deal had proven an enormous success. Once the convertibles were redeemed, I rarely thought about it at all. Certainly, it never occurred to me that a transaction remarkably similar to the one we had done with Siegler Collery would eventually destroy Geotek and lead to my own forced resignation.

CHAPTER SEVEN

CORE TECHNOLOGY, CORE INVESTORS

By the beginning of 1994, the number of employees Geotek's budget supported, either directly or indirectly (as in the case of the subcontracted Rafael group) was in the low hundreds. Our monthly burn rate had ballooned to around $2M, and though Bogen had become profitable, its earnings were miniscule compared to the expenses of our much larger wireless division. Though we still had a comfortable cushion of cash in the bank, it was clear to me that we would soon need much more. Already, our original estimated development costs seemed ridiculously low, and I was beginning to realize that even the real R&D expenses would likely be dwarfed by the price-tag for setting up a national push-to-talk/cellular FHMA network. It was time, in other words, to raise capital again.

The good news was that the financial markets were quite strong, and the cellular field, in particular, was hot. In Europe, GSM was in the final stages of approval as the sole cellular standard (though the regulatory status of digital specialized mobile radio remained unclear). In the U.S., however, everything was still in the air. Most major providers had yet to settle on a digital technology, and their eventual choices were the subject of intense speculation among investors. Despite the fact that wireless service had been offered in the U.S longer than anywhere else, the local industry was far from mature, and savvy investors realized that better than anyone. For the next few years, companies like Geotek would find themselves in a sellers' market, though not nearly to the extent that dot-com companies would enjoy in the late 1990s.

My first encounter with the financial community's enthu-siasm for the type of innovative development Geotek was doing came one day early in 1994, when I met with PC Chatterjee, who managed virtually all of George Soros's tech-nology investments. Earlier that morning, I had received a call from Gary Fuhrman, Geotek's investment banker, inform-ing me that Mr. Chatterjee wanted to meet with me right away. It was a highly surprising invitation, to say the least, as Geotek was still a small company, and both Soros and Chatterjee were anything but small investors. I had little time to think about it, however, as I quickly rescheduled my appointments for the day and rushed into the city.

PC Chatterjee, a brilliant investor with a strong background in both technology and business administration, was the founder and president of the Chatterjee Group, a moderately sized but very influential private equity fund. The reason for the PC's influence was simple: aside from administering the Chatterjee fund, he also managed George Soros's personal investments in high-risk technology companies. No one knew for sure how much money Soros had allocated for these type of investments, but it hardly mattered. For Chatterjee, the fact that one of the most successful financiers of his day had cho-sen to place his faith in him provided all the credibility he could ever need. In fact, part of the arrangement between Chatterjee and Soros was that the breakdown of the funding for any investment was never revealed to outside parties. It was impossible, therefore, to distinguish between the funds that came from Soros and the money from other Chatterjee investors, which worked to the advantage of both men.

My presentation to Chatterjee and his analyst, Jim Pete, was somewhat improvisational, as I had not had time to prepare written material or slides. The two men's thorough understanding of technology, however, made it easier to present my pitch. As the meeting went on, and I continued to field increasingly detailed questions from Chatterjee and Pete, I began to wonder what kind of an investment I should request. When the issue finally came up, several hours into the meeting, I explained that our goal for that round of financing was to raise a total of $40M, and suggested that the Chatterjee Group invest a quarter of that sum, or $10M. The response to my request was as swift as it was surprising: his fund needed no partners for that kind of investment, Chatterjee told me. Assuming their due diligence revealed no major issues of concern, they would prefer to contribute the entire $40M themselves.

A few weeks after my meeting with Chatterjee, Gary called me about another potential investor, Vanguard Cellular, a small cellular service provider with about $250M in annual revenue from networks in Pennsylvania and Florida (it eventually merged with AT&T Wireless in the late 1990s). Like Chatterjee, Vanguard's top executives became very enthusiastic about Geotek, and shortly after I met with them, they made an offer to invest $30M in the company, under terms that were similar, though not identical, to the ones that Gary and I were already negotiating with the Chatterjee Group.

One principal difference between the offers, aside from their sizes, was that Vanguard's called for only part of the money be released immediately, with the rest contingent on a proof-of-concept demonstration of FHMA (which was to be completed by mid 1995). The other unique element of Vanguard's offer was a much more positive one, from our perspective. Vanguard agreed to provide Geotek with operational help and guidance on issues such as designing and implementing a comprehensive billing system, building technical and customer support infrastructures, and so forth. Though these were hardly the most pressing tasks Geotek had to contend with, and were certainly not the sexiest, they were crucial issues with which we could certainly use the help.

Since both offers Geotek received were quite strong, the company's board decided to increase the size of its preferred stock issuing and accept them both. Together, the deals netted Geotek $70M and added two new directors to its board: PC Chatterjee, representing both his fund and George Soros, and Haynes Griffin, Vanguard's Chairman and CEO.

The twin investments by the Chatterjee Group and Vanguard Cellular transformed Geotek into a market star. The involvement of Soros, in particular, provided an enormous boost to the company's profile in the financial community. The memory of his successes in the currency markets earlier in the decade was still fresh in the minds of many investors, and, as a result, Wall Street closely followed his every move. Partly as a result of this buzz, Geotek was able to raise another $100M within a year. Of that sum, half came through two additional $25M preferred stock investments by Soros and the Chatterjee Group, the first in late 1994; the second, early the following year. Also in the first half of 1995, Geotek raised $50M from the Claridge and Renaissance funds. Renaissance was a small venture capital fund created by Charles Bronfman to invest in companies with an Israeli orientation or connection. It was intimately related to Claridge, a much larger company that was essentially a private investment fund for the Bronfman fortune. Of the $50M the two funds invested, $10M came from Renaissance, with the rest originating from Claridge and its related interests. The deal Geotek negotiated with the two funds was nearly identical to the ones that had been made with Chatterjee, the only difference being that Claridge and Renaissance did not request representation in Geotek's board of directors. Over the years, they proved to be remarkably "hands-off" investors, though I did stay in touch with Jonathan Kolber, the head of Renaissance, and occasionally updated him on Geotek's progress during my visits to Israel.

Geotek was never an easy company to run. It seemed, sometimes, as though we were always in the throws of at least one crisis. In the early 1990s, it was the constant threat of a cash crunch that was my biggest concern. In later years, network deployment problems took center stage. From early 1993 through mid 1995, however, Geotek's focus, as well as my own, was on navigating the obstacle course that was the development of our core technology.

The infusion of cash from Chatterjee and Vanguard allowed PST to move its operations to a higher gear. One of the biggest beneficiaries of this was Rafael, which saw the size of its FHMA group skyrocket. What had started out as a small project became one of its most lucrative contracts. At a time of government cutbacks, it also provided Rafael with positive local news coverage and a generally higher profile in the civilian Israeli business world. For these reasons, Rafael went out of its way to try to accommodate Geotek and PST and meet their unique needs. It gave PST the use of prime real estate on its corporate campus, streamlined a significant portion of its countless regulations, and at least considered our requests at the highest level of management.

Nevertheless, there was no getting around the fact that Rafael was a *dinosaur*, with a bureaucratic apparatus that was just awe-inspiring. Though the organization was well known in Israel, many did not realize that it was not a standard government-owned company (like, say, the National Electric Utility), for the simple reason that it was not, technically, a company at all. It was a *unit* of the Ministry of Defense, which made it, in some ways, more similar to the Shin Bet or Mossad, which are units of the Prime Minister's Office, than to Israel's many government-owned corporations. As a result of this unique structure, Rafael was highly prone to internal political in fighting, which was extremely disruptive to the operation of PST, particularly since so much of the actual development work was done by Rafael directly, as a PST subcontractor. For all their good intentions, the brass at Rafael ultimately saw PST as just another customer, one that they did not have to satisfy all the time. When necessary, us could be used as a bargaining chip. At the very least, our requests could be processed in a leisurely fashion when resources were needed for more politically important projects, or when it was unclear who would get credit for our successes or failures. PST was a strategically important customer, but Rafael had plenty of other issues with which it had to contend. For Yitzhak Gat, who became the CEO of Rafael in 1993, the biggest of these was the mission he had taken upon himself of finally turning the organization into a regular government-owned company.

Many of Israel's political and business leaders were highly supportive of Gat's objective. Some saw it as a first step in the eventual privatization of Rafael, which could free the government from the financial burden of supporting the frequently money-losing organization. The biggest obstacle to Gat's plan was the opposition of Rafael's highly powerful, politically connected employees' union. The union did not oppose the change in principal, but it demanded a contract that would guarantee Rafael's employees the same generous benefits package that they received as employees of the Ministry of Defense, which included early retirement eligibility, paid sabbaticals, protection from downsizing, and so forth.

As a result of the tension between Rafael and its employees, PST suffered from a problem that inflicts few technology companies – a strike. Though none of PST's employees were involved, they were unable to enter their offices without crossing the picket line. To its defense, the union was aware of PST's importance to the continued viability of Rafael, and quickly agreed to allow PST's employees into the compound without heckling or threats. The bigger problem, however, was that at least half of PST's effective workforce was made up of Rafael's FHMA group, so while development work did not grind to a halt, it came extremely close to it.

Aside from the strike, there were countless other moments of friction in the relationship between PST and Rafael. Many of these could have been avoided had David Tamir, PST's CEO, acted more diplomatically. The problem was not that he was disliked by his former colleagues; overall, the relationship between David and the project managers at Rafael was friendly enough. When it came to business matters, however, he was as stubborn as he was demanding, and was capable of making his former colleagues' lives absolutely miserable on account of relatively minor delays, inefficiencies or missed details. One issue that was a typical trigger for altercation was documentation, which was a point of weakness for some Rafael engineers. While PST (and Geotek) certainly needed proper FHMA documentation, we did not need it so urgently that it was worth disrupting development. Inevitably, once an argument escalated into a full-blown crisis, I would be asked to mediate between PST and Rafael's management, since David was all but incapable of agreeing to a compromise, and the executives at Rafael were usually too furious to deal with him directly anyway. Partly as a result of this, I became increasingly involved in development throughout 1994-1995, and participated in all the design review meetings, coming to Israel on a monthly basis. It was hardly an ideal situation, as it created some grumbling among the developers that I was making decisions that were beyond the scope of my technological understanding. Ultimately, however, the developers needed my help in dealing with Rafael more than anyone, so they came to accept my intimate involvement.

One of the reasons the development of FHMA was so complex was that the project included both hardware and software elements. Initially, both Geotek/PST and Rafael viewed the project mainly from the hardware perspective. The heart of the mission, as we saw it, was to design two "boxes" – a subscriber unit and a network base station (technically, each of these "boxes" consisted of several disjoint parts. The subscriber unit contained a dashboard module and a module stowed in the car's trunk. The base station consisted of a server loaded with proprietary cards, an antenna controlled by power amplifiers, and various additional pieces of hardware, such as power supplies). As development moved forward, however, it became clear that the design and implementation of the software that ran the system as a whole was a far greater challenge than that of the hardware (which included implementing the basic operating software as well, but not the applications necessary to support real user functionality). This was an unfortunate discovery for us, since Rafael's core strengths were more pronounced in hardware design than in software development.

Perhaps the biggest difference between the hardware and software related challenges that PST faced was that with hardware, the requirements were so much easier to define. Fundamentally, two hardware issues needed to be resolved, and though their solutions were technologically complex, they were also predictable. They required work and ingenuity to figure out, but the basic approaches needed for solving them were clear from the start.

The first challenge was to design frequency hopping equipment that would comply with the FCC's radio frequency (RF) emissions regulations for SMR use in the 900 MHz spectrum. This was a difficult proposition both because Rafael's technology was not originally designed with the civilian market in mind, and because Geotek's macro-cellular approach naturally implied that base stations (and, to a lesser extent, subscriber units) would need to transmit at high power. Nevertheless, PST and Rafael were able to come up with methods to keep transmissions within the allowed parameters. Once the emission mask hurdle had been overcome, we still needed to figure out how to build base stations at a reasonable cost. This proved easier than we had feared, however, as PST found ways to lower the price tag of an FHMA base station from $300K to around $60K.

With the hardware issues solved and the basic FHMA operating software functional, Geotek was able to meet a critical milestone that Vanguard Cellular had mandated as a condition of its investment in us. The Vanguard test, as it came to be known internally, was a proof-of-concept demonstration that had been designed to show the capacity capabilities of FHMA. In order to perform the test, PST put up a base station prototype in the Carmel Mountains near Haifa. We had yet to build a real mobile phone, so a temporary subscriber unit, or TSU, was used instead. The TSU was a hulking, rather ugly prototype of the "guts" of a commercial subscriber unit. It was not exactly a phone, but it did communicate with an FHMA base station the way a mobile phone would. In the first step of the test, the TSU was driven around the Carmel and a call was simulated, by transmitting data between the TSU and base station, under ideal conditions. In the second step, we added a source of interference to the mix, and the experiment was repeated under various levels of "noise." The results, in both cases, were highly positive. The second part of the test, in particular, showed that FHMA was as capacity-efficient as CDMA. It was an important moment for Geotek, and it symbolically marked the end of the "core technology" development stage. I certainly could not imagine, that day late in 1994 that I would come to see the period that preceded it as the "easy" one.

CHAPTER EIGHT

THE BEGINNING OF A DIFFICULT TRANSITION

In 1992, when Geotek first got into the wireless business, it told its investors that its network, GeoNet, would be launched sometime in the second half of 1995. Though there had been some early development delays, we began the year still hoping to achieve, or at least nearly achieve, that initial schedule. With our successes thus far, most notably in attracting strategic investors and with the Vanguard test, I believed there was good reason to be optimistic. Several major tasks, however, remained to be completed before we could begin to roll out GeoNet. Perhaps the most urgent of these, to my mind, was developing our network's subscriber equipment, namely, car phones and back-office dispatch workstations. It was an issue about which Dr. Oliver Hilsenrath, Geotek's CTO, and I disagreed, as he believed that developing the subscriber equipment would be relatively simple and could be put off for a few months while we worked on other things. Since he had little experience with the end user world, however, I decided to trust my instinct that the development of the car phone, or commercial subscriber unit (CSU), would be a more difficult undertaking than Oliver predicted. Shortly after the Vanguard test, therefore, we created a new group at PST that was charged with designing GeoNet's CSU.

The core of the CSU was to be based on the temporary subscriber unit (TSU), which had been built by Rafael as a test unit and was used primarily to assess the performance of the FHMA base station. Significant parts of the CSU, however, had to be developed from scratch. Given the difficulties PST had encountered on the Rafael campus, and the inherent differences in the expertise needed to develop a subscriber unit and a base wireless system, I decided to locate the new operation in a separate location. I settled on the Israeli town of Petach-Tikva due largely to its central location, which, I hoped, would make it easier to attract the most qualified experts in the relevant fields. The Petach-Tikva group, as it became known internally at Geotek, was charged not only with working with PST and Rafael, but also with coordinating its efforts with two new Geotek companies charged with developing our wireless data application. The first, GMSI, was a company we had recently acquired, based in Ontario, Canada, that sold mainly to police departments and taxi fleets. The second, MIS, was a joint venture we formed with Decision Systems Israel (DSI), an established software developer. I asked Tamir Friedrich, a childhood friend whom I had brought to Bogen a few years earlier, to head the CSU development effort. It was a promotion for him, as it brought him into the center of the "action" at Geotek, and he handled his new responsibilities very well, navigating countless obstacles to oversee some of Geotek's the most important technological achievements. Later on, I even asked Tamir to Replace David Tamir as the General Manager of PST in Israel. Nevertheless, the position put a heavy strain on our personal relationship, and our friendship never fully recovered from it. I always loved Tamir and had great respect for him as an individual and a professional. I consider the unraveling of our close relationship a big personal loss.

Despite all the effort, GeoNet's subscriber equipment, like other aspects of the network, was not ready in time. As 1995 progressed, it became increasingly clear to me that some of the challenges Geotek had taken upon itself were simply too great. With the CSU, for example, one of the most difficult tasks we faced was miniaturization. It was an area in which our engineers, for all their ingenuity, had little real-world experience. At a time when tiny handheld phones were starting to dominate the cellular, though still not the SMR, landscape, I knew this was a major weakness, one that would only be exacerbated once phones went into production. Clearly, we were in need of some major outside help.

In spite of the development difficulties and delays, the focus of Geotek's operations began to shift towards marketing, sales and network deployment logistics the closer we came to our predicted launch date. Though it was clear by the spring of 1995 that we would not be ready to launch GeoNet that year, we still believed that the initial group of major metropolitan networks could be up and running by sometime in the first quarter of 1996. As a result, Geotek's American organization experienced a huge growth spurt. We had ended 1994 with a little over fifty employees in our wireless division, all but a handful of whom were based in NJ. By the end of 1995, we had at least three or four times that number, located in perhaps a dozen locations. Almost overnight, without having sold a single service contract, Geotek went from obscure startup to a company that, though hardly a household name, was on the radar screen of nearly everyone who shopped for SMR services. The industry, in spite of Nextel's meteoric growth in the preceding years, was still highly fractured and technologically primitive. Even Nextel, with its seemingly inexhaustible supply of capital, was plagued by significant service and technology problems, epitomized by a lack of capacity that left users furiously pushing their push-to-talk buttons when searching for a line. The message Geotek received from its potential customers, therefore, was a highly encouraging one. Fleet administrators, and the corporate bosses to whom they answered, were eager for an alternative to the analog SMR services they were getting, particularly if it allowed for data communications as well as voice. We found that the "C3" concept - command, control, and communication - taken from the military, was particularly appealing to commercial decision makers responsible for transportation, delivery security and other such fields.

One of my biggest regrets regarding Geotek has been the ambitiousness of our deployment plan. From the start, we intended to roll out service, simultaneously, in over a dozen major markets, including New York City, Philadelphia and Washington DC. Furthermore, we intended to offer at least some data applications as soon as service was launched, though we had yet to decide which ones, or how sophisticated we would try to make them by the launch. I also believed, however, that it was imperative that we begin offering service as quickly as possible. The growth of Nextel, whose business plan was ultimately very similar to Geotek's, was an element on which I had not counted. They were ahead of us in nearly every respect: customer base, spectrum ownership, name recognition, etc. I feared that if we did not launch soon, it would become that much harder to compete.

The more days slipped away, the more convinced I was that time-to-market was crucial, and that boldness, rather than caution, would continue to serve Geotek as it had in the past. What I did not realize, however, was that the race we were trying to win was not real. We were competing with our own impossible timeline, and with Wall Street expectations that were largely the result of unrealistic projections coming from us as well. In reality, the market was still very far from maturity and far less competitive than I led myself to believe. While Nextel had grown quite big, there was still an enormous base of potential subscribers who were either unhappy with the quality of their service or were simply untapped. With Nextel's momentum growing, however, I believed we had to take off soon or forever lose our opportunity to depart the figurative runway.

With this in mind, both Geotek's board of directors and I came to believe that the company needed to change if we were to meet the challenges ahead. We had to transform our character from that of a small high-tech company to that of a wireless service provider capable of dealing with the enormous organizational complexity of managing all aspects of a thirteen-location constantly operating system. We needed new departments, such as sales and customer support. We needed a much more sophisticated marketing operation. Even seemingly simple things, ones to which I had never given too much thought, suddenly became challenging.. We needed a billing system, for example, that was order of magnitudes more sophisticated than any enterprise system we had used thus far. It had to be capable of communicating with the proprietary, still incomplete software that ran the FHMA base stations and of keeping track of yet-to-be-determined services used in yet-to-be-defined zones under a yet-to-be-determined roaming price structures. Individually, none of these changes was overwhelming. Taken together, however, they required Geotek to transform the way it operated.

The first step to doing this, I decided, was to fill some key positions at Geotek. During 1995, I hired, for the first time, a few senior officers with significant experience in the service side of the wireless industry. These new executives brought not only a new - and different - point of view to Geotek, but also a more corporate style, one that was, in many way, at odds with the earlier, less formal and less hierarchical, culture that had developed at the company. It was a transition that was both painful and necessary, one that had its successes and its failures. As with so many other managerial challenges, the difference between failure and success had at least as much to do with the quality of leadership as with the specification of objectives.

The first of this new group of executives join Geotek was Bill Opet, whom I hired as our Senior VP of Sales. Opet was a cellular industry veteran, who had begun his career in the field at Lin Cellular, the first independent service provider in the New York region (i.e. the first provider in the area not owned by the local telephone company). After Lin was acquired by McCaw Cellular, Opet joined McCaw and held a number of increasingly senior posts in sales and marketing. At Geotek, he provided the kind of down-in-the-trenches know-how that we desperately needed. He was a charismatic, intelligent, and very skillful salesperson, with a real understanding of what it took to build an effective sales organization in his chosen field. What he lacked, however, were the "people skills" necessary to do this without stepping on others' toes. Too often, in his zeal to achieve milestones, he pushed his subordinates too hard. In the long run, this hurt both him and Geotek far more than if he had simply come to me and asked for more time or resources for his team. Nevertheless, Opet's contribution to Geotek was very significant. His biggest task, overseeing the rapid creation of a national sales organization, was an unenviable one, and he did it well, starting from the time that he joined Geotek and through the launch of GeoNet in late 1996.

Prior to hiring Opet, I had interviewed a man by the name of Mike McCoy, a former executive at a long-distance company, for the Senior VP of Sales position. Though I decided I could not give McCoy the job, since he lacked experience in the cellular field, I was very impressed by him and was reluctant to deprive Geotek of such a talented and versatile individual. As a result, I offered McCoy the position of VP of Marketing, reporting to the recently hired Bill Opet. He stayed in the job less than a year, however, as he was promoted to CFO in early 1996, when Yoram Bibring became the head of the Geotek International group and left the CFO position open. By 1997, McCoy was Geotek's COO, in charge of nearly all aspects of our U.S. network's operations. He made a noticeable contribution to Geotek by establishing well defined business processes in almost every part of our U.S. business.

The most crucial of 1995's "new generation" of Geotek employees, however, was Jonathan Crane, a former executive at MCI who had headed their Northeast business with P&L responsibility for over $2B. Much of the rationale for Crane's hiring, late in 1995, as Geotek's President and COO, was to give the company a strong organizational man, someone with the type of experience in a large corporate environment that I simply did not have. Unlike most personnel decisions, the hiring of Jonathan Crane, which entailed the creation of a COO position that previously had not existed in any meaningful way at Geotek, was discussed at great length by the board of directors. The goal, which, eventually, we were forced to scale back, was for me to hand over to Crane the vast majority of the responsibility for Geotek's day-to-day operations. I would remain actively in charge of financing as well as strategically important issues such as product development, business partnerships and the international networks, but everything else was to fall under the COO's scope of responsibilities. In conjunction with this, I was also given the position of Geotek's Chairman of the Board (partly because Win Churchill, who had just started SCP, a new venture capital fund, was trying to decrease the amount of time he needed to devote to Geotek).

Crane made some positive structural and procedural changes at Geotek, and was initially greeted with enthusiasm both within the organization and, especially, by financial analysts, who understood the magnitude of the challenges we faced. Soon, however, it became clear that much of the job simply was not getting done in an acceptable manner. Crane handled many of his individual responsibilities well, but he had trouble seeing the greater picture. Just as crucially, he did not truly "lead" the organization with which he was charged, and certainly did not inspire his employees (or, for that matter, our investors). He was by no means a terrible COO, but he had been hired at a time when Geotek needed an outstanding one. When we fell upon hard times, about a year after Crane joined the company, he just was not up to the task of managing the crises at hand.

CHAPTER NINE

BUYING UP SPECTRUMS

From my first meeting with Irvin Gross in late 1991, when the idea of Geotek as a cellular service provider was born, it was clear that the fate of the project would rest on our ability to secure appropriate frequencies in key markets. In the U.S., that meant acquiring SMR licenses *in the 900 MHz range* in as many of the major metropolitan areas as possible. We needed at least a megahertz in each major market, or 500 KHz in smaller ones, to be able to support enough subscribers to give the networks a realistic shot at profitability. This was a tiny amount by cellular industry standards, as providers typically own around 30 MHz worth of frequencies in each major market, but, with FHMA, it was enough to allow Geotek to support thousands of subscribers in each market it served. One aspect of the frequencies was crucial, however: they had to be in the 900 MHz range. It was not the technology that dictated this requirement, but the circumstances of the frequency market. The American SMR spectrum consisted of 10 MHz per market in the 800 MHz range but only 2.5 MHz in the 900s. The 800 MHz frequencies had been allocated in the early 1980s and were in the same range as the initial cellular spectrums. The 900 MHz license, on the other hand, were given out only in the early 1990s. As a result, they were still relatively underutilized and inexpensive. This was in no small part due to the fact that Nextel, whose planned digital technology required large continuous spectrums, was buying exclusively in the 800s. It therefore made a good deal of financial sense for Geotek to develop its technology for the 900 MHz range, from which we could actually afford to "shop." Since the size of the spectrum allocated for SMR use in this range was so small, however, it meant we had to be smart in our acquisitions: we could not afford to pay too much, but there were some frequencies we simply *had* to have if we were to compete on that national stage.

In 1994, as Geotek was just beginning to purchase spectrum licenses, a major deal, which had an enormous impact on the SMR industry, was announced by Motorola and Nextel. Its crucial element was the sale of Motorola's SMR licenses to Nextel in exchange for stock in the company and a long-term commitment from Nextel to use the iDEN (MIRS) platform. It was not a trivial decision for Motorola to make, since the SMR frequencies had been a reliable source of income for the company for many years, but they decided to gamble on Nextel's long-term success in the hope of strengthening their core wireless equipment business. Needless to say, it was a smart decision. The partnership, a marriage between two of the biggest names in SMR, was a major setback for Geotek, as it strengthened our biggest future competitor, Nextel, both in terms of frequency ownership and technology. Though there was nothing we could do to stop the deal, we did fight to lessen its impact by playing a big roll in a Justice Department investigation against the two companies. We worked with DOJ officials for a long period of time, helping them reach the conclusion that Motorola and Nextel were monopolizing the industry through their control of both the vast majority of the SMR spectrums and the only available digital radio technology for SMR. This resulted in a consent decree, negotiated between the DOJ and Nextel and Motorola, which limited the amount of SMR frequencies they could control in any major metropolitan area. This consent decree forced Nextel to divest some of its 800 MHZ and 900 MHZ licenses, which allowed Geotek to significantly improve its position in certain important markets. We put a lot of work into the DOJ initiative, and it proved to be a great way of showing the world that we would not be pushed over by the big guys, and that a small, innovative, entrepreneurial company could influence decisions made in Washington. I am sure that if the administration at the time had been a Republican one, however, the issue would not have gotten the attention of the Anti-Trust division at the Justice Department.

In late 1993, I was approached by Lee Dixon, a Washington, DC based broker who represented a local SMR provider looking to sell a 250 KHz license in a hurry. In a typical analog scenario, the license could support ten simultaneous push-to-talk calls, each utilizing 25 KHz (an industry standard for reasonable voice quality in a non-compressed system). With FHMA's projected thirty time capacity improvement, however, a 250 KHz spectrum could allow for as many as three hundred simultaneous calls, potentially supporting thousands of subscribers. The price quoted by the broker for the SMR license – a hundred thousand dollars – was exceptionally low, but it came with a caveat – the offer was good for twenty-four hours only. Despite the unusual condition, and the limited resources Geotek had at the time, I decided we should jump on the deal. It was a good decision, as eight months later a similar license in Washington, DC cost us $500K, and by the next time we purchased a license in the city, a year later, the price had risen to $1M. Though Geotek's first frequency acquisition involved only a small amount of money, it was a big deal for us, because it made an important statement. It showed that we were confident in our chosen path of leveraging the FHMA technology build a commercial network and become a service provider.

Shortly after the first license purchase, a team at Geotek created a prioritized "wish list" of frequencies covering most major markets in the U.S. In the couple of years that followed, we continued buying licenses from small regional SMR service providers on an opportunistic basis, as they became available. As had been the case in Washington, license prices rose rapidly in cities around the country as SMR providers increasingly came to realize that the changing nature of the wireless business meant their radio frequencies were far more valuable than they had ever been before.

One of the most difficult markets in the country to acquire spectrum licenses was Metropolitan New York City. This was a critical obstacle for Geotek, one that both I and many of our investors began to worry about early on. New York was important not only because of the sheer size and wealth of its potential customer base, but also because of its location at the center of the Northeastern corridor, which was crucial to our plans for the future. If GeoNet could not establish a presence in the Northeast, the most lucrative part of the country, it would be difficult to convince anyone that our aspiration of becoming a serious player on the national stage, a real competitor to Nextel, was a serious one.

Early in 1994, I learned that Metro Net Systems, a private radio provider whose network covered mostly Long Island but also Manhattan, had come on the block. By far the most attractive quality of the company, from Geotek's perspective, was their ownership of two 250 KHz licenses in the 900 MHz spectrum in New York City, plus a significant number of 800 MHZ licenses. Though the number of 900 MHZ licenses was small - certainly not enough for a large FHMA network – I decided that, given the difficulty of finding frequencies for sale in the city, we could not afford to let the opportunity pass us by. It was a testament to Geotek's desperation for spectrum licenses in Manhattan that our board of directors, at my urging, agreed to pay $30M, in Geotek stock, for Metro Net, which had received several offers from other parties, including Nextel. We also agreed to give Richard Frantz, Metro Net's CEO, a position in Geotek's board of directors, and to continue providing analog service to Metro Net's 12,000 customers.

Geotek's first opportunity to buy a significant quantity of spectrum licenses at once came late in 1995, when a Scandinavian-owned cellular and paging service provider called Milicom decided to liquidate its American business. The frequencies owned by Milicom were all in sections of 900 MHz spectrum licensed for SMR use. Equally as attractive, however, was the fact that Milicom had obtained a waiver from the FCC of the licenses' "construction deadline." This deadline, which was associated with nearly all SMR 900 MHZ frequencies in the U.S., stipulated that the frequencies had to be used to provide a commercial wireless service within a short timeframe from the date of purchase. This waiver was given to Milicom because it was presumably developing advanced new wireless data applications meant to enhance its standard paging services. Although Geotek was not automatically eligible to keep the waiver when it bought Milicom's spectrum license (for $15M), we were able to convince the FCC to grant us that privilege since we also intended to use the frequencies for new data application (along with voice communication). Furthermore, because of the ambitious nature of our plans, the FCC agreed to let us apply the waiver to most of our other existing and future licenses as well. This decision was of significant importance to Geotek, and it was a major victory for Mike Hirsch, our regulatory representative in Washington, who had made it a priority. Had he not been as successful in lobbying the FCC for the new waiver, we might have had no choice but to begin providing analog SMR services in at least some of the markets in which we owned frequencies. Given how complex the Geotek organization had already become, adding this extra facet to the company would have been a difficult burden, both from a financial and human resources perspective.

Although the Milicom licenses had helped solidify Geotek's holdings of spectrum licenses, we still entered 1996 with a few major holes. Nextel had been acquiring licenses voraciously over the preceding couple of years, and though it preferred 800 MHz frequencies to 900 MHz ones, its presence in the market made all SMR spectrums much more expensive, and competitive, than they had ever been. While Nextel and Geotek were now the two biggest buyers in the market, there was still plenty of interest from other parties as well, which made every license acquisition a struggle.

For every potential buyer in the market, from the smallest regional providers to Geotek and Nextel, there remained one eagerly anticipated opportunity to acquire new, electro-magnetically "clean" 800 and 900 MHz frequencies – the FCC's SMR auction scheduled for early 1996 (This was the smaller of the two FCC auctions that took place that year. The other, the PCS auction, was the first government offering of new cellular licenses since the 1980s. It was a massive success, bringing in billions of dollars to the U.S. treasury and allowing two new providers, Sprint and T-Mobile, to enter the competition for cellular dollars on a nationwide basis). The SMR auction was scheduled to take place over a period of two weeks under a complex, strict set of FCC guidelines. A special team at Geotek, formed months in advance and comprised of personnel from both technical and marketing and sales departments, was charged with preparing our bid. Its biggest priority was obtaining more frequencies in New York and a few other critical cities. For these markets, the instructions the team was given were clear: they were to bid to win, no matter what the cost. For other regions, the bids were more opportunistic, based on projections of future needs and resale values.

The announcement of the FCC auction's results was a major milestone for Geotek. We had submitted the winning bids for all our "must have" licenses, and won many additional frequencies throughout the country as well. In the final tally, we owed the U.S. government just about $30M, a significant sum, but one that we could afford. There remained only one major market in which Geotek did not own any spectrum licenses – Los Angeles. We were left with some "holes" in a few other cities, but those were fixable, though at an exorbitant cost. In San Francisco, for example, we purchased a 250 KHz SMR license in a $2M stock deal. It was a ridiculous price – twenty times what we had paid for a similar license less than three years earlier in the bigger city of Washington - but we had little choice but to accept it. Failure to obtain the frequencies would have meant delaying our launch in San Francisco indefinitely, or launching a network that could not provide an acceptable level of service to a sizable number of subscribers.

Geotek's success in acquiring spectrum licenses was important for the company not just because we needed the frequencies to launch GeoNet, but also because it gave us a great deal of credibility with stockholders and investors. As the sums we sought to raise grew increasingly larger, often into the nine-figure territory, it was no longer enough just to show promising technology and a compelling vision. At that level, investors wanted proof that we had the ability to make things happen on the ground, outside the lab or office. Geotek's ability to obtain the critical electro-magnetic infrastructure for a national network in such a short timeframe, and for a very reasonable price, went a long way towards convincing potential backers that we had what it took to pursue a goal that was exceedingly ambitious for such a small company.

CHAPTER TEN

INTERNATIONAL VENTURES

Geotek's first foray into the international commercial wireless market occurred with our 1993 acquisition of the UK provider National Band Three (NB3) from Vodafone. It was an opportunistic deal, as we had not set out to expand outside of the U.S. so early, but it was in keeping with my earliest strategic vision for Geotek (from the post-Rafael-partnership period) of bringing FHMA to SMR markets throughout the globe. Gary Fuhrman, of A&SB had called me one day saying that Geotek should try to buy the SMR network owned by Vodaphone. To this day I don't know if it was his original idea or if Vodafone had put the company up for sale, but a couple of days later I found myself on the Concord with Gary, going on a day trip to London to see if NB3 could be acquired. After a two hour lunch meeting with the CEO and CFO of Vodafone, we agreed over a handshake to buy the company for $25M. Though we were still in the early stages of developing our technology when we took over NB3, we did hope that in the years to come we would be able to convert its analog network to FHMA. In the meantime, we found ourselves with our first subscribers. NB3's 30,000 customers were our earliest in the wireless field by far, preceding the first American GeoNet subscribers by a full two years.

Although NB3, a money-losing SMR provider with few immediate prospects of being allowed to provide cellular service, was rather "unsexy" for a wireless company, it proved to be a very good investment for Geotek. Even without making any major technological changes, we were quickly able to turn it around and begin showing customer and revenue growth. It also helped us several times over the years in securing financing, both because it was a saleable asset and because it demonstrated that we were capable of successfully running a large scale commercial wireless service organization.

Emboldened by the relative ease with which we were able to absorb NB3, as well as by an emerging but still highly unformed European SMR standard known as TETRA, we acquired and merged together two small analog private radio providers in Germany. Each had had only a few thousand subscribers, and both had struggled financially because of their small sizes. The merged company was also too small to enjoy real economies of scale, however, so shortly after the acquisitions were completed I approached our biggest competitor in the region, a provider owned by RWE, the main electrical power provider for the Rhine district, and suggested another merger. Our spectrum licenses were highly complementary, I reasoned, and while Geotek had more subscribers, RWE's subsidiary owned more equipment. We agreed, therefore, on a 50/50 ownership structure in the merged provider, which would now be able to offer coverage to a significant portion of Germany's population.

Although both our German and UK networks entered the right track and began experiencing growth under Geotek's watch, our hopes of converting them to FHMA and using them as the launching pad for a European GeoNet did not pan out. In hindsight, I view these hopes as insufficiently thought out and a little naïve. The biggest obstacle we faced was that European regulators, unlike their American counter-parts, generally believed in uniform, well-enforced standards. Realistically, the only way that Geotek could have brought FHMA to Europe would have been by influencing the TETRA standard. There were far greater forces than us already trying to do that, however, and though we made a few half-hearted attempts to showcase FHMA as a possible model for TETRA, it quickly became clear that we were out of our league. More crucially, however, we just always had more pressing issues that needed to be resolved, especially as the launch of GeoNet neared in 1996 and, a year later, when we found ourselves faced with a major cash crunch.

The strategy we had adopted for our European networks exemplifies Geotek's internal conflict between being a network operator and an equipment provider. We did have the option to team up with either Motorola or Alcatel and subscribe to a plan to deploy TETRA, the European standard, in our UK and German networks. Such a plan, which could have been financed separately from Geotek, would have made us the first provider of digital SMR services in Europe. Certain executives from Motorola approached me more then once with the idea of making us the "Nextel" of Europe but our strong desire to make FHMA the technology of choice for digital SMR made us decline these overtures and give up on a great opportunity. Eventually, in late 1997, we were forced do sell our European networks due to financial pressures related to our U.S. operations. We had over 100,000 subscribers in the continent by that point.

Geotek's most ambitious and complicated international venture began in late 1995, when I was contacted by Jim Kim, a Korean-American billionaire based in Philadelphia, regarding the possibility of bidding together for a license to operate a nationwide SMR network in South Korea. Kim's company, Amkor Semiconductors, which was the largest semiconductors packaging company in the world, had little experience in the cellular world. It was, however, a well-financed and highly-regarded corporation with a large Korean subsidiary, ANAM Semiconductors. This domestic connection was crucial, as the terms of the Korean government's offering made it clear that the successful bidder would be owned largely (though by no means entirely) by local partners. As part of this new partnership, Amkor invested $10 million in Geotek.

The Korean license offering attracted attention from cellular, technology and communications companies around the world for one exceedingly simple reason: it was *not* an auction. At a time when countries everywhere were selling spectrum licenses for hundreds of millions, and in many cases, billions, of dollars, the Seoul government was offering valuable 800 MHz frequencies free of charge. The offerings primary condition, other than a commitment to building a national network and the financial strength to back up this obligation, was technological superiority – both in terms of voice quality and advanced data features. It was an example of the South Korean government's strong support over the last 15-20 years for innovative technologies. Qualcomm, for instance, owes a great deal of its worldwide success to the willingness of the Korean government to take a chance on CDMA before any other country would.

After some negotiation with Kim, as well as internal technological evaluations and research into the conditions in Korea, Geotek agreed to form a joint venture with ANAM. ANAM Telecom, as the venture was named, was funded entirely by ANAM but relied completely on Geotek's technology. I was never very happy with our share of the company, just 20%, but ANAM had insisted that any greater stake by a foreign company would doom the joint venture's chances of winning the Korean government's favor. Geotek's investigation into the matter in the weeks after Kim first contacted me, an admittedly brief and not-entirely-comprehensive one, yielded inconclusive results. It was likely, it seemed, that we could have gotten away with owning a bit more of ANAM Telecom, but the legal and political circumstances surrounding the offering were somewhat murky. Either way, entering the race in Korea was strategically a no-brainer for us, as the opportunity to compete for free licenses, not to mention major international exposure, was far too attractive to pass up. Also, like other Western companies that had partnered with Korean ones, we figured there would be plenty of profit opportunities for us in the future – primarily from selling equipment and support – if our bid was actually chosen. That, however, was a rather enormous "if."

To describe ANAM Telecom as an underdog among the bidders would be a major understatement. The groups we competed against featured some of the biggest and most successful names in the cellular world, such as Ericsson, Motorola and Alcatel, as partners. These were companies whose equipment was used daily by many millions of subscribers. Geotek, in contrast, had perhaps fifty or sixty thousand subscribers worldwide. More to the point, none of our networks used FHMA or, for that matter, any other digital technology. In fact, Geotek's first demo site was just being constructed at the time ANAM Telecom submitted its bid, and not a single non-prototype FHMA subscriber unit (let alone a *handheld* phone) had even been produced.

They say that when the Gods want to punish you, they make your dreams come true. I often think about that when reflecting on Geotek's Korea adventure. The announcement of ANAM Telecom's unlikely success was received with a euphoric reaction from Geotek's employees and management. To their credit, however, the financial markets were wary of the news. The major investors seemed to understand that the deal would put tremendous additional pressure on the already overextended Geotek organization. I had hoped for a sharp increase in our stock price after the announcement, but that did not happen. The stock, in fact, barely reacted to our press release at all.

Once the initial excitement had worn off, Geotek was left with a vast new set of responsibilities. First and foremost among them: FHMA had to be adapted to the 800 MHz spectrum. From a technological point of view, it was not *too* difficult a task, since the propagation pattern of waves in the 800 MHz range is similar to that of 900 MHz waves. The problem was that our engineers at PST and Rafael were already working under enormous pressure. The launch of GeoNet in the U.S. was behind schedule and nearly every day brought about fresh bug discoveries. The last thing I wanted to do was divert experienced developers away from finally finishing everything that had to be done to make the core FHMA platform stable enough for commercial use. But I had no choice. Geotek had committed, to the Korean government and ANAM, that the network would be up and running in less than a year's time. Our reputation, not to mention our financial well-being, was now inextricably tied to the project. Even if they had not been, however, I was hardly willing to give up on one of Geotek's greatest triumphs. The difficulties we faced were just something we had to live with and overcome, I believed.

The situation in the U.S., meanwhile, was only slightly better. While the Korea challenges were mostly technological, the corporate organization also had to support ANAM Telecom and divert time and effort away from our upcoming American launch and its crises. We opened an office in Seoul to coordinate between ANAM Telecom, PST, the Korean government, and other involved parties. I asked John Moon, whom I had originally hired for Bogen in 1992 and then transferred to Geotek in 1994, to head our Korean office. John had advanced quickly at Geotek, due to his talent, good nature, and general ability to get things done. Under John's leadership, Geotek's Seoul office grew rapidly, eventually reaching more than thirty employees from both Geotek and Rafael. Years later, I hired John again to work with me and with some of the companies in which I had invested.

One of our first tasks in Korea was to analyze and map the physical conditions, such as topography, population density, radio interferences and so forth, of the areas the Korean network needed to cover. Luckily, since about 80% of Korea's business activity takes place in Seoul, Busan, and the corridor between the two cities, the country proved much easier to cover than the U.S. We found that it was possible to effectively provide coverage for the vast majority of the national market by designing high-capacity networks in just the two critical cities, plus the highway that runs between them.

Towards the end of the first quarter of 1997, PST completed adapting FHMA to the 800 MHz spectral range. The work had been done on schedule and with great success, and, with base station priced at about $250K each, Geotek was well on its way to recovering the projects' cost and even making a profit.

To assemble and support the FHMA base stations, ANAM Telecom sub contracted Hyundai, one of Southeast Asia's biggest industrial conglomerates. Since Geotek did not want to reveal too much proprietary information to Hyundai, however, we sold the stations in the form of semi-knocked-down kits, or SKDs, which were essentially disassembled base stations provided with detailed assembly instructions. In addition, Hyundai began to develop subscriber units for ANAM Telecom, relying on PST's Petach-Tikva group for help. As it became acquainted with FHMA, it grew very enthusiastic about its commercial potential and even suggested to Geotek that we form a strategic partnership in order to pursue joint opportunities, an offer we were delighted to accept (in particular, Hyundai hoped to bring FHMA to the Chinese market). I was invited to Korea for the signing of the strategic partnership agreement early in 1997, in an elaborate and well-publicized ceremony attended by the top management of Hyundai Electronics. On that same trip, Jim Kim took me to see the Korean Minister Of Communication, who expressed his support for our venture and his enthusiasm about bringing new technology into the Korean wireless market. Unfortunately, nothing more came of Geotek's relationship with Hyundai, as we soon hit upon a financial crisis that eventually led to our bankruptcy and liquidation.

In early 1997, Anam Telecom started the construction of its FHMA network in Korea; later that year, it began selling wireless services to commercial customers around the country. The network grew to become a successful venture that continued to operate, with Rafael's help, long after Geotek was no longer around. I remember receiving a phone call from John Moon, in 1999, telling me that he had just come back from Seoul, where he had seen an FHMA unit in service in the cab that took him from the airport. As insignificant as this phone call was, it was, for me, a small vindication of our vision and technology.

In the years since Geotek's collapse, I have come to view my decision to aggressively pursue international expansion opportunities as a mistake, one symptomatic of a general tendency to try to accomplish too much too quickly. As it turned out, Geotek's international investments were some of its most lucrative. We sold our European networks late in 1997 for $107M, an immense profit, and had also begun to make some money in Korea, especially on the sale of base stations. All of these international properties, however, were a significant drain on our limited human resources, and they contributed to Geotek's complex, even convoluted, corporate and financial structure. The effect was to make it that much more difficult for us to concentrate on our core business of building and operating an FHMA commercial wireless network in the U.S. Ultimately, we just could not do everything at once, but by the time I finally realized this, the tide had already begun to turn against us.

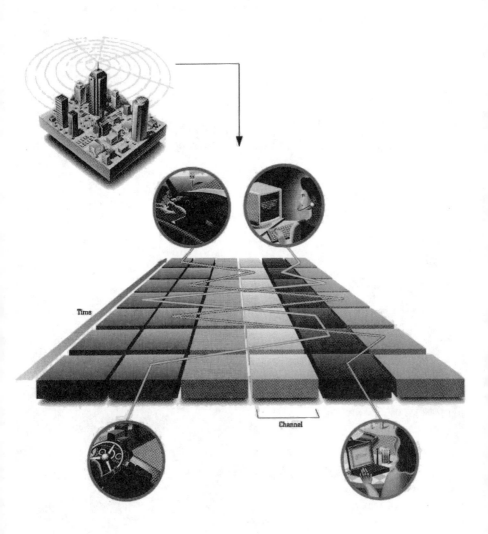

In a Frequency Hopping system each voice or data transmission is divided into short bursts of digital information, which are transmitted over a number of radio channels. Each burst is transmitted over a different channel according to a special hopping sequence at the rate of 250 bursts per second. The sequence is unique to each transmission, and decipherable only by the transmitter and receiver involved. The hopping algorithms allow for a controlled frequency range, resulting in significant gains in traffic capacity and security over a relatively small band of spectrum.

Geotek's digital mobile radio network will deliver advanced productivity-enhancing services including telephony and dispatch, messaging, credit authorization, vehicle location, and a host of mobile data applications, all running on one easy-to-use Mobile Workstation.

The Geotek "work station for the road" featured telephony and dispatch capabilities as well as multiple data applications such as vehicle location tracking, two-way messaging and credit card authorization

In anticipation of a major re-launch in March of 1998 Geotek embarked on a positioning campaign that included revamping its logo.

Geotek's 1998 re-launch was accompanied by a major media campaign managed by Bright Sun Consulting, which created this full-page ad that ran in *Business Week*. Ads also ran in the *Wall Street Journal* and the *New York Times*.

CHAPTER ELEVEN
A RACE AGAINST TIME

With GeoNet's expected launch date rapidly nearing, I began 1996 on the road, trying to raise additional capital for what was sure to be an expensive year. The hot financial instrument of the moment on Wall Street was junk bonds, and given that the sum Geotek was hoping to raise, $125M, was so large, we decided to pursue this type of financing. It was the second attempt we made to issue junk bonds. The first had taken place just six months earlier, with Lehman Brothers and Bear Stearns as our underwriters. Our goal had been to find buyers for bonds bearing a 10% annual interest rate. After a three-week long road show, however, the best offers we received involved an interest rate of 15%. Servicing that kind of debt would have placed an enormous burden on Geotek, so the Board of Directors and I decided to withdraw the offering. This failed bond offering was a somewhat traumatic experience for the company, since we had worked very hard on it and had little to show for our efforts. It was with some hesitation, therefore, that we considered the issue again late in 1995. I was approached, this time, by Solomon Smith Barney, a large and diversified investment bank that was a novice in the junk bond field. The market for high yield bonds being as strong as it was, however, they were eager to make a splash with a big offering, one that would show the financial community that they belonged in the big leagues. As a result, Solomon Smith Barney made Geotek an offer that was hard to refuse. They would put their best people on the project, they promised, and would make the utmost effort to secure for us a better deal than our previous underwriters had done. The team working for Geotek would be headed by Bob Lessen, one of the firm's Vice Chairmen. It was an enticing proposal, since Geotek had been a relatively "small fish" for our previous bankers at Lehman Brothers and Bear Stearns, so we decided to accept it and begin the process of trying to find investors once again - with Smith Barney as our sole underwriter this time.

Geotek's 1996 road show was largely based on the one we had done a few months earlier. It covered mostly the same cities and our audience even included some of the same potential investors, all of which were large institutional funds. This time, however, the bankers and I were joined by several key people from Geotek, including George Calhoun, who was one of my closest advisers at the company and was well respected by market analysts; Bill Opet, who spoke about our sales plans; Andrew Robb, the CEO of NB3; and, of course, Yoram Bibring, Geotek's CFO, who had been present in the first road show as well. While the reception we received was generally positive, Geotek's fundamental riskiness had not changed since our earlier, aborted offering, and we were still a hard sell for bond investors. One of the biggest challenges was finding a lead investor, a respected party that would be willing to buy at least 20% of the issued bonds, and whose reputation would make it easier for other funds to invest as well. After much consideration, Solomon Smith Barney recommended that we approach Merrill Lynch's

Global Allocation Fund, which was managed out of Princeton, NJ by Bryan Ison. Ison agreed to become the lead investor for the offering if the bonds were secured by Geotek's physical assets, including its spectrum licenses and the European networks, which could easily be sold off if the need ever arose. To cover standard operating expenses, we would be allowed to spend only about half of the money raised through the offering. The rest could be used only for infrastructure-related investment. It was a difficult restriction for me to accept, since I knew that most of Geotek's expenses in the near future would be operational. Nevertheless, I decided to recommend to our board that we accept Merrill Lynch's terms. With that decision made, Solomon Smith Barney was then able to find additional investors, with a great deal of additional effort, and close the $125M offering early in 1996. The bonds' yield, at 13%, was higher than we had hoped, but it was within the range we deemed acceptable. In spite of the compromises, the debt offering was viewed by both Wall Street analysts and the press as a major success for Geotek.

Over the years PST worked with Rafael, I had become increasingly uncomfortable with the idea of Geotek relying solely on the agency to manufacture equipment for it. This was partly because Rafael's prices were a little on the high side, but mostly because I wanted GeoNet to have the backing of a much bigger vendor with experience in the civilian wireless field. Also, from a broader perspective, I did not want Geotek to rely so heavily on any company.

The equipment GeoNet needed fell into four main categories: off-the-shelf items, such as servers, power supplies and antennas; proprietary base station components, such as computer/electronics cards and power amplifiers; proprietary end-user equipment, such as subscriber units and handheld phones; and telephone switches, which, while not proprietary, required significant customization.

For the latter requirement, Geotek had already found a temporary solution, in the form of a PBX switch made by an Israeli telecommunication equipment maker called Tadiran, which we subcontracted to do the basic integration work as well (as part of the deal for providing us with the "mobile switch," the company also agreed to invest $3M in Geotek). The PBX switch was more suitable for a large internal phone system, such as might be used by a corporate center or a hotel, than for a sophisticated national network with data and push-to-talk functionalities, but it was sufficient to get us started. The more urgent problem, however, was finding a vendor to make our *proprietary* equipment, particularly the subscriber units, which we could not even ask Rafael to manufacture since they were being developed directly by PST's Petach-Tikva group.

Finding a company to manufacture FHMA equipment for GeoNet proved to be quite difficult. The main problem was that while the network's needs were quite small by industry standards, the start-up costs associated with launching an entirely new production line were very high. For companies such as Ericsson, Lucent, or Nortel, all of which we either approached or at least considered approaching, the amount of business Geotek could potentially generate simply did not justify the effort or risk inherent to working with a new technology like FHMA. They were already busy supplying equipment to networks that utilized thousands of base stations and supported millions of phones, so the prospect of even a hundred million dollars worth of potential orders (over a several year period) was just not that big a deal. At one point, we even met with Dr. Ed Steiano, the head of Motorola's General Systems Sector, which was in charge of most of the company's cellular business, to discuss the possibility of Motorola manufacturing FHMA equipment for Geotek. Dr. Steiano told us that they made one million cellular phones *a month*, and would have little interest in a project in which that number of units might only be reached after several years.

Since we were too small to appeal to the biggest telecommunications equipment makers, we had no choice but to approach a second-tier company. Nevertheless, it had to be an organization that we could trust, one with a longer track record in the wireless industry than we had. Late in 1995, George Calhoun suggested that we approach a company he knew from his years at IMM to see if they might be a suitable vendor for us. Hughes Network Systems (HNS), a unit of Hughes Electronics (a division of General Motors) was a mid-sized company whose core business was supplying satellite equipment to large corporations and government agencies. As I quickly learned, however, it was extremely eager to increase its activities in the bigger terrestrial communications market. HNS's experience in the cellular industry was limited, but not inconsequential. They were the main supplier of cellular phones to GM. Most of these units were car-phones, which were well-designed if not all that technologically sophisticated, but they had also made a handheld model. It was not a great phone, but it was a decent one, and it showed that HNS was capable of making acceptable equipment. We were not looking for a vendor to develop our core technology, after all, just for a partner with manufacturing and product design capabilities.

Geotek signed its first contracts with HNS early in 1996. One of the biggest advantages of HNS from our perspective was that they viewed their partnership with us as a strategically important one, as they saw it as a way of gaining visibility in the cellular world and building their reputation as a terrestrial communications equipment maker. As a result, shortly after we began to work together, HNS agreed to extend to Geotek a five year $100M vendor credit facility with a 10% interest rate. It was an enormous show of confidence on their behalf, and constituted our second biggest financing deal to that date. We ended up using only about half of the credit line, however, partly as a result of the nature of our previous financing deal. Since much of the equipment we bought from HNS was considered "infrastructure," we were allowed to pay for it with the restricted portion of the $125M we raised by issuing junk bonds. Geotek had few other infrastructure-related expenditures by this point, so it made financial sense to divide the payments to HNS between the two sources of capital. After all, Geotek had far more money in the bank then it needed for infrastructure expenses, while, at the same time, our burn rate was almost $10M per month.

We bought two types of equipment from HNS: handheld phones, which HNS developed out of its San Diego facility in close cooperation with PST's Petach-Tikva group; and base stations, which were manufactured, based on Rafael's pre-existing specifications, at HNS's main facility near Washington, DC. To its credit, the HNS development group that worked on the handheld phone did its work quite quickly under less than ideal circumstances, as the subscriber unit that they based the phone on was still in development in Israel in early 1996. It was a significant achievement, therefore, when HNS was able to deliver the first batch of phones roughly nine months after the design work had begun. The base station product line took longer for them to set up. It was not until the second quarter of 1997 that all the kinks had been worked out and Geotek was able to start buying base stations from HNS instead of Rafael. As a result, of the 200 or so base stations that GeoNet eventually had, only the last fifty were purchased from HNS. Nevertheless, once HNS got production up and running, they were a good supplier for us, easier to deal with, in many ways, than Rafael.

The last remaining piece of the puzzle, as far as procuring proprietary equipment went, was finding a manufacturer to build the vehicle-based subscriber units being developed in Petach-Tikva, which were designed to support GeoNet's advanced data capabilities and were our central piece of end-user equipment. In conjunction with the units' development, PST built a small manufacturing facility in the town of Yokneam in Israel. The initial cost of making each car-phone, however, was astronomical – about a thousand dollars. To effectively compete in the marketplace, GeoNet could sell the units for no more than $200 apiece. It was clear, therefore, that we had to reduce their cost dramatically. To a certain extent, this could be done in-house, and the Yokneam facility did eventually succeed in bringing the per-unit cost down to $350. To reduce the costs further, however, we needed a partner with more experience and a greater potential for benefiting from economies of scale. Since the subscriber units were so technologically complex, however, we did not want to rely on HNS. Instead, Geotek made a deal with Mitsubishi. My initial contact with the company was with their headquarters in Japan, where we were treated with a great deal of respect but were given few financial breaks. Nevertheless, Mitsubishi looked like a very good partner for us, and we signed a deal with them a few months after the agreement with HNS had been finalized. One of Mitsubishi's most attractive qualities was that a couple of years earlier they had been involved, with Bell South and IBM, in the creation of an ambitious wireless data product known as SIMON. SIMON was in many ways a product ahead of its time, and it flopped horribly. As a result of the failed project, however, Mitsubishi had acquired a great deal of expertise in the wireless data field. The flip side, on the other hand, was that they were extremely cautious about their wireless activities, making it difficult to work with them.

While Geotek negotiated its deal with Mitsubishi's corporate office in Japan, the actual work was to be done by the company's American subsidiary in Atlanta, GA, where Mitsubishi's analog and TDMA cellular phones were made. As we soon discovered, however, the people who ran the Atlanta facility had virtually no discretionary authority. Whatever Geotek requested had to be approved by the powers-that-be in Japan. There was no deliberate attempt to be uncooperative towards Geotek, but the end result was that we had to be involved in the manufacturing of subscriber units on a much more hands-on level than I would have liked, particularly when it came to speeding up the procurement of parts. Eventually, though, the production problems were worked out and the quality of the equipment we received was good. Of the roughly 30K-35K mobile subscriber units GeoNet sold, around 25K-28K were made by Mitsubishi, with the rest coming in from PST's production line in Israel.

At the same time that Geotek was working to build a supply chain of commercial equipment, we also began our initial network deployment, relying on prototype base stations and subscriber units. The first city we entered, in late 1995, was Philadelphia. The opening of our office in the city was accompanied by a good deal of public relations fanfare, since the city was to serve as our main demo site for the U.S. Our main macro-cell transmitted from One Liberty Place, the city's tallest building, a picture of which appeared on the cover of our 1995 annual report. The office Geotek opened in Philadelphia was a fairly big one, since it had to accommodate not only sales, marketing, and operations personnel, but also a number of PST and Rafael employees who came to assist with the installation and troubleshooting of the network equipment.

The first few months of the Philadelphia network's "beta" operation were some of the most challenging Geotek faced. Almost immediately, it became clear that the macro-cellular model on which we had based many of our plans and predictions was hopelessly flawed. While the approach was valid, for the most part, in theory, it was untenable in real-world situations. The problem, as it so often was in the wireless world, was topographical. Our macro-cell simply left too many holes with little or no coverage. When one tested coverage with a handheld phone, rather than a car-phone, the situation was even worse. Instead of being able to transmit at 3W, the phone was now limited to 1W. Our hope with FHMA had been that we could avoid many of the costs and complexities of a full-blown cellular system, most of which had to do with the massive construction requirements of such systems and the need to devise handoff protocols to handle transitioning between a large number of overlapping cells. We expected our network would require only one large cell and a few small ones to take care of the trouble spots. In reality, however, the areas in which we needed additional cells were so numerous that it became more accurate to view the macro-cell as just one of the several dozen cells needed to adequately cover a major metropolitan region.

Though the discovery of FHMA's limitations was a set-back, it was not so much the technological aspects of the problems that bothered me, but the logistical ones. We had enough money by this point that we could afford to buy the extra base stations and fix the handoff protocols. What we did not have, I believed, was time. The more we kept putting off GeoNet's launch, the more worried I grew that our chance was slipping away. I pushed everybody at Geotek, and especially those at PST (and Rafael), as hard as I possibly could during those months, trying to get every issue resolved in as short a time as feasible. Getting *anything* done quickly, however, became more and more difficult as Geotek expanded and its partnerships multiplied. We opened offices and built base stations in about a dozen cities in 1996. Every time a bug was fixed, or a new part had to be installed, or some configuration needed to be altered, the necessary changes had to be performed for each base station or each subscriber unit. Our system was designed to have the capability to deliver automatic updates, but, in those early months, the feature had yet to be implemented. As a result, GeoNet needed to perform the tasks manually, which was particularly problematic when it was the vehicle-installed subscriber units that required updating. Bug fixes and new features also had to be coordinated with HNS and Mitsubishi, since they were building the same type of units we were busy repairing. Our resources, in other words, were just spread too thin. In spite of all these problems, however, we soon embarked on an ambitious shift in strategy that added a great deal of strain to the already overextended Geotek organization.

By the middle of 1996, we had missed our projected launch date by over six months, and the financial markets were becoming increasingly anxious. It was widely feared that the delay in launching GeoNet was causing Geotek to lose momentum, and that if we did not make a splash soon, it would be impossible for us to regain that momentum. In hindsight, I believe this fear was over-exaggerated, that our race against time was largely an unnecessary one. At the time, however, I was, for the most part, persuaded by Wall Street's analysis of our situation. In an effort to best prepare GeoNet to position itself for its launch, I decided to seek some outside advice.

We settled on the small, "boutique," consulting firm of Malarkey-Taylor, which was based in Washington, DC and had a good deal of experience advising the wireless industry. The firm's analysis of our situation led it to present us with the following recommendation: GeoNet, they suggested, should be positioned at either the extreme low-end or the extreme high-end of the wireless provider spectrum. If we chose the former option, we could sell our product as a "poor man's cell phone," a kind of low-cost extended cordless phone, which could be used around the subscriber's neighborhood and would have no roaming capabilities or advanced functionality. If we chose the latter option, on the other hand, we would need to present GeoNet as a network offering unique communication services for the mobile worker. That would mean offering advanced, integrated data applications, features that none of our competitors offered, from the very start. Support for data communication had always been a major part of Geotek's plan, of course, but what Malarkey-Taylor was suggesting was far more ambitious. To be the provider of choice for the mobile worker, GeoNet would need to offer subscribers more than just general data capabilities; it would need to offer complete, attractive data application, ones that would allow users, and the businesses that paid their bills, to increase their productivity in a meaningful way.

Geotek immediately rejected the "neighborhood cell phone" option, which was, in many ways, the antithesis of what we had been trying to accomplish from the very start. One reason was that we had a limited number of spectrum licenses, and knew that we had to find a way to maximize revenue from them. Another, equally important, reason was that our goal had always been to build an advanced network that would appeal to commercial customers more concerned with quality than with price point. We aspired to be the wireless world's IBM, not its Wal-Mart. What the analysis done by Malarkey-Taylor indicated to us, however, was that our technology required further development before we could position GeoNet the way we envisioned it. It was a sound conclusion, but our response to it was far too extreme. We decided to immediately put the development of data applications into high gear in order to get them ready for GeoNet's launch later that year. It was a ridiculously ambitious goal, given that PST and Rafael were already working at full capacity just to debug the FHMA system and increase its reliability. Nevertheless, I believed it was what we had to do and what we could do, if everyone just gave it their best effort.

Though most of the work was already on its way, much of it was still at a relatively early stage, and its sudden fast-tracking was a major burden on Geotek. Technology products, particularly software, often have a development cycle that is extremely difficult to accelerate beyond a certain point. At the end of the day, only so many developers can work on the same project before overall productivity is diminished. There are just too many tasks that must take place sequentially. It is of little use, for example, to begin testing an application before it is fully coded. Similarly, starting to write code before a basic system architecture is defined often leads to more delays than it prevents. To accelerate the development of the top level data architecture, we hired Kolnet, an engineering firm in Tel Aviv whose founder and manager, a man named Pitsi, was known as an expert in the field. The firm's role was to design the overall data architecture for the FHMA system and to show Rafael and PST the changes they needed to implement to accommodate the new capabilities. In retrospect, I believe we designed a state of the art wireless data network that envisioned the revolutionary shift in data communication technology, over the succeeding few years, from Circuit Switched to Internet Protocol (IP) based. I see this as an example of how right Geotek was in understanding the long term trajectory of wireless technology and applications. Nevertheless, we did not help ourselves by pushing development so forcefully. The developers, most of whom belonged to either our Canadian subsidiary, GMSI, or our Israeli joint venture, MIS, did a fine job. So did the data applications group in our U.S. headquarters, which was charged with the crucial task of devising integration solutions for potential customers, mostly large, corporate ones, interested in linking Geotek's applications to their internal enterprise systems. In spite of everybody's efforts, however, the pressure on development had devastating consequences for GeoNet once the network was launched.

One unfortunate result of GeoNet's delayed launch was that while much of Geotek's workforce was swamped with work, many of the company's employees had little to do but idly stand by. Starting in late 1995, Bill Opet began to assemble sales teams in each of our initial launch markets. At the same time, John Egidio, our VP for U.S. Operations, supervised the creation of a massive logistical infrastructure in each of the markets. We opened regional offices, hired technical and non-technical support staffs, rented space for base stations, contracted with the local phone companies for T1 lines, and secured transmission rights for the antennas we needed to put up throughout the areas we would cover. We also increased both human and technological resources in our corporate office to handle issues such as billing, customer support, human resources, and so forth. Geotek's burn rate increased dramatically. By the end of 1996, it was close to $10M a month. Equally as damaging, however, was the waste of employees' time. Large swaths of our workforce simply did not have enough work to do. The recently hired salespeople were particularly demoralized, since they had expected their salaries to be significantly augmented by commissions. Even for those who were not hurt financially, however, it was frustrating to have so little to do.

Despite the fact that Geotek was beginning to spend money at an alarming rate, the financial markets were not overly worried. In fact, one of our easiest financing rounds occurred in the summer of 1996. We had no immediate need to raise capital at the time, but the market was hot, and Bob Lessen, the Vice Chairman of Solomon Smith Barney, who had headed the team that managed Geotek's bond offering, suggested we should take advantage of the favorable market conditions. He recommended that we issue preferred, fixed-priced convertible stocks, an instrument that was in high demand by many investors. Unlike the previous offering, which had required representatives of Geotek and Smith Barney to go on a road show, the convertible offering was done entirely through a series of conference phone calls. There was a great deal of enthusiasm among potential investors about Geotek's decision to focus on value added services such as data applications, and Smith Barney had little trouble filling their book with the names of interested investors. All told, we raised $75M in the offering, for a total of $300M in new financing throughout 1996 (including the vendor credit deal with HNS). We began that year's third quarter with nearly $200M in the bank. In spite of all the problems Geotek had encountered over the year, there was good reason to be optimistic.

CHAPTER TWELVE

LAUNCHING PREMATURELY

In October, 1996, GeoNet was finally launched, and it was a disaster. The network came online, almost overnight, in half a dozen of the country's biggest markets, and it just was not ready. Coverage was riddled with holes; subscriber units were unstable; the hastily developed dispatcher software was sluggish and prone to crashes; and GeoNet's valiant but inexperienced technical support staff was overextended and incapable of providing subscribers with the kind of service they deserved. Because the launch had been delayed for so long, many of our customers were already familiar with the network's end-user equipment and its capabilities, having been thoroughly exposed to demo systems by GeoNet's salespeople. These were customers who had signed up in advance, early adopters who were eager to take advantage of our technology's most advanced features. In nearly any industry, the initial customers are crucial, since their impressions have such an enormous influence on the larger public's perception of the product. Our customers expected a state-of-the-art SMR network, and that expectation made their disappointment all the greater. It was, without a doubt, Geotek's biggest crisis thus far.

There were two principal reasons for the failure of GeoNet's launch: firstly, we had not deployed enough base stations; and secondly, the subscriber units and back-end customer software had not been sufficiently debugged. They were essentially "alpha" or "beta" releases, and their behavior in uncontrolled situations was unpredictable.

Unfortunately, there was no way for Geotek to un-ring the bell and take the launch back. By the time we realized the extent of the problems, several weeks after GeoNet began operations, we already had a about two thousands active subscribers all over the country. Their wide distribution made the situation especially difficult to manage. There was no way to isolate the crisis - we had to deal with it everywhere we were.

About a month after GeoNet's launch, we announced the freezing of all new sales until the network's technical problems were resolved. It was a drastic move, but one which we had no choice but to make. To entice customers to stay, we credited them for all their costs through April, 1997, giving them free air time until the network was finally re-launched. In the meantime, Geotek drastically increased orders for base stations and intensified its debugging efforts, especially for the end-user terminals and dispatcher stations. There was no magic bullet we could turn to in order to resolve GeoNet's predicament; the problems simply had to be solved. I came to visualize the network as a piece of Swiss cheese, full of holes; countless small issues, combined with a few larger ones, made the overall structure highly unstable. The only way to repair the system was to plug in the holes, one by one. We had tried to make shortcuts, and now we were paying the price.

Though some of the responsibility for GeoNet's failed launch certainly rested with me, a good deal of the blame belonged to Jonathan Crane, who, as Geotek's President and COO, had direct responsibility over the network during the period up to and immediately after the launch. As a result, shortly after the launch was halted, I decided to take over most of Crane's duties as COO. We came to an agreement whereby we swapped some of our responsibilities. I became Geotek's de-facto COO, overseeing damage-control and reconstruction at GeoNet, while he took over supervision of PST and Geotek International.

Shortly after we switched roles, Crane made one additional mistake that was indicative of his shortcomings as a senior manager, and eventually sealed his fate at Geotek and led to his resignation a couple of months later. The incident took place in my office, during a conference call with shareholders and Wall Street analysts. In answering an analyst's questions, Crane mentioned that GeoNet had received orders for 25,000 subscriber units and service contracts. When asked whether these orders were firm, he responded with a statement that, while ambiguous, nevertheless made it seem as though they were. In fact, we had only gotten confirmations of *intent* for purchases totaling this size; there was nothing legally binding about most of them, and no money had changed hands. Fortunately, I was able to correct the erroneous impression created by Crane's statement in a response to a later question posed during the call. I had no idea, at the time, how important this correction would end up being for us. In the end, it was one of the main reasons that not even a single class action lawsuit was filed against Geotek after it declared bankruptcy. The fact that we were always honest with our shareholders made it impossible to make an effective case against us for misleading investors.

───··──

The months after GeoNet's launch were some of my most difficult at Geotek. For the first time since the early 1990s, I began to seriously fear for the company's future. One bright spot, however, was our continuing success in securing financing. The business model Geotek had chosen was an extremely capital-intensive one, far more so than I had ever suspected. Nevertheless, it had been years since we had had any real difficulty raising capital, and the future looked good, from that perspective.

In December, 1996, just a few weeks after we halted GeoNet's launch, I had a fateful meeting, in our Montvale, NJ offices, with Bob Lessen, the Vice Chairman of Solomon Smith Barney. During our conversation, Lessen made one bold prediction. In the upcoming year, he told me, the market would choose winners from losers in the wireless field – and once that happened, investors would have no more interest in small players such as Geotek. In other words, if we wanted to survive, we had better assemble a "war chest" while it still could.

Whether Lessen's analysis was ultimately correct or not, I did take it to heart. He was one of Wall Street's savviest rising stars, and his argument certainly seemed convincing. When I discussed the possibility of another round of financing with Gary Fuhrman, the banker who had engineered several of Geotek's earlier financing deals, he recommended that we use an instrument that had been very successful for us in the past – the preferred, variable-priced convertible. It was the instrument we had used to raise capital for the acquisition of NB3 – the first time Geotek had raised "institutional" money. Given that it was nearly impossible for investors *not* to make a profit from variable-priced convertibles, Gary was confident he would have no difficulty quickly finding investors for us if we chose to pursue that type of financing. His confidence was well-warranted – investors buying this unique instrument are betting only that the company in question stays in business as a publicly-traded company and remains liquid. As long as these modest conditions are met, it is all but impossible for them.

Shortly after I spoke to Gary, Geotek's board had a series of long, detailed discussion about the idea, during which it evaluated the proposed financing structure. At the end, the decision was made to go forward and raise capital using preferred variable-priced convertibles. Though some of the directors were well-known financial experts who were very much aware of the risk associated with this kind of financial instrument, they decided to recommend it nevertheless. One of Geotek's board members, PC Chatterjee, even decided to invest $30M in the offering, on behalf of both George Soros and his own fund.

Our initial goal for the offering was to raise $80M. The demand for the convertibles was so high, however, that we ended up raising a total of $130M. It was the biggest round of financing in Geotek's history – and its last in times of good financial health. Our investors this time around were very different from our past backers. With the exception of Chatterjee and Soros, all seven of them were hedge funds – hardly a typical kind of strategic investors. At the time, neither I nor any other major figure at Geotek read too much into this fact. It should have raised a red flag for us, however. If it had, maybe thing would have turned out differently for the company. The offering was closed in the first quarter of 1997, when our stock was trading for about $10 a share and the company's market–cap was approximately one billion dollars. A year later, both numbers would be reduced to a fraction of these values.

In April, 1997, GeoNet started selling service and equipment again. It was a "soft" re-launch, done intentionally with little fanfare and publicity. We wanted to avoid overwhelming our still fragile network, and make sure that the various fixes that had been implemented were properly working before we made any more bold promises. Slowly but surely, however, both sales and network quality picked up. Between the fall of 1996 and the soft launch of April 1997 we had nearly doubled the number of base stations in all major markets and significantly improved the quality of both the subscriber units and data applications. By summer, we were signing up thousands of subscribers a month. It was nowhere near what Nextel was doing, of course, but the numbers were solid. Just as importantly, customer satisfaction was high. Customers were especially pleased with the data applications the network offered. As many as 80% of them purchased at least one data-related feature, typically the GPS-based vehicle tracking and dispatching system. It was an enormous percentage, and a real validation of Geotek's strategy of positioning GeoNet as a provider of value-added services, of features that no other network could deliver. The customers we were able to attract were not just typical SMR customers. We negotiated deals with well known companies like Airborne Express, PepsiCo, Time Warner Cable and many others who decided to use Geotek as the main communication and content provider for their fleets in different parts of the country. Airborne Express, for example, eventually had over five thousands vehicles using the GeoNet solution in the New York Metropolitan area alone. We also began to receive very positive press coverage from industry media, which often depicted GeoNet as a value added service provider, unlike Nextel, which was perceived as a more cellular-like provider.

A month or two after the re-launch, Jonathan Crane re-signed. I appointed Mike McCoy to replace him as President and COO of Geotek USA, in charge of managing the continuing deployment and growth of our U.S. network. I, meanwhile, went back to concentrating once again on our long-term strategic plans. Chief among these was the launch of a major new marketing and repositioning campaign for GeoNet, one that would serve as a kind of "hard" re-launch for the network itself - and propel it back into the public's awareness as the most advanced network of its kind.

CHAPTER THIRTEEN

RUNNING A BIG COMPANY

I started Geotek's wireless division, in the summer of 1992, with a small team of just five people. As the nature of our business changed, we experienced rapid and prolonged periods of growth; by 1997 I found myself managing an organization of twelve hundred people with offices in seven countries. These numbers only hint at the complexity of Geotek's business, however, as the challenges of overseeing a large organization can hardly be measured in revenue or the number of employees alone. Factors such as the maturity of the organization, the diversity of issues that require a CEO's close attention, the company's monthly burn rate, and its geographic distribution contribute to these challenges as well. I suspect that there are companies that generate hundreds of millions of dollars in revenue and employ thousands of people but do not pose as great a managerial challenge as Geotek did.

By 1997 Geotek was burning about $11M a month - more than your average startup company raises and spends in its entire lifetime. A burn rate of this magnitude places an enormous burden on management to execute its plans quickly, as every month of delays comes at a huge price tag. As a result, I put tremendous pressures on the Geotek organization to stick to counterproductive timetables, not only because of our competitive situation but also to optimize use of capital. Operating outside the plan became a common and acceptable way of accomplishing tasks, and I routinely approved millions of dollars in additional spending to deal with delays. It is common wisdom that time-to-market is key for a company trying to establish itself with a new technology in an existing market. With Geotek, I learned the hard way that this is true only to a point, as there are only so many shortcuts you can take before the journey becomes effectively longer instead of shorter. The technological and operational shortcuts that Geotek took made it weaker in the long run, and because we burned through cash so quickly as we struggled to keep to our schedule, the task of raising capital became the centerpiece of my agenda. I believe now that I should have defined less ambitious, and less time and capital-intensive, objectives for Geotek.

I became seriously worried about our cash position only in late 1997 into early 1998, after our stock price collapsed, and though I took some steps to limit expenses, it was too late in the game for truly radical cuts. With GeoNet gaining momentum, and the Korean network coming along nicely, our fixed costs were astronomical. When we tried committing less money to building subscriber units, for example, we created shortages in the field. Similarly, when we delayed deployment of new base stations, customers complained that we were not addressing coverage problems quickly enough. An additional source of complaint was the size of the support staff, which we could not afford to increase as the subscriber base grew.

I began finding a huge pile of checks waiting to be signed on my desk every morning, along with a stack of messages from suppliers anxious to collect. I had daily meetings with our CFO to decide which payments to make that day and which we could hold off on for a bit longer without causing the company too much pain. Dealing with angry vendors became the most dreaded and unpleasant part of my daily routine.

Most startup companies focus on delivering either a new technology or a new service to the market. Geotek tried doing both, each on a massive scale. We developed our core technology, built base stations, and designed and built mobile phones and data terminals all while constructing and operating wireless networks in the U.S. and abroad. The diversity of activities created an unusual challenge for me and the rest of our management team. I worked long hours during my last couple of years at Geotek, typically arriving at the office by 7 AM to a day filled with meetings covering a wide variety of issues: wireless data applications; accounts payable and cash flow; pricing strategy and major proposals; customer service issues; and network performance and production related problems. In addition, I was constantly involved with regulatory issues related to the FCC, personnel decisions, and complex legal matters related to the hundreds of agreements Geotek had signed over the years. By the end, we had eighty-eight registered subsidiaries, each representing some kind of a distinct operation or activity. In addition, I continued working to raise capital virtually every day of my tenure at Geotek. The diversity of issues was extremely wide, and I was later blamed by colleagues for being too involved in too many of them, for knowing too much but not listening enough. Partly this was the result of the way issues grew so much more complex over time. I remember turning to Yoram Bibring once, after an especially difficult meeting, to comment that I missed the old days when finding solutions to the problems we were facing had seemed so much easier.

━━‿ • ‿━━

In addition to a good management team, organizational structure, operational processes and company tradition are some of the keys to solving complex managerial issues. One thing that I do believe I did right was to recognize the need to build a solid organizational structure and develop the processes necessary to achieve results. I instituted major structural changes at several points in Geotek's history, the most significant of which occurred in 1996-1997 with the creation of Geotek USA as a wireless service provider, Geotek Technologies (PST) as a developer and producer of FHMA technology and equipment, and Geotek International as a separate subsidiary (headed by Yoram Bibring) in charge of our non-U.S. networks. After the restructuring, Geotek USA became an independent subsidiary with its own management team charged with, among other tasks, negotiating the acquisition of equipment and services from PST. It developed detailed processes for sales, installation and customer support of FHMA equipment and services. The company employed over 600 people and became the heart of Geotek as we had always envisioned it. Geotek Technologies (PST) was given the mandate to develop and produce FHMA equipment and sell it to Geotek USA, Anam Telecom in Korea and other unrelated customers. Perhaps the most innovative group of Geotek, in the end, was the wireless data group, headed by Bill Opet. With about a hundred developers working on the design and customization of cutting-edge wireless data applications, it was the only group in Geotek whose work was not exclusive to FHMA, as we believed the applications had great potential for integration into other types of networks as well.

I believe that we did build an organization that was quite strong despite the mistakes made in staffing some of its key positions. One major potential source of strength that Geotek lacked, however, was tradition. Strong steel is created in a very slow cooling of liquid iron, a process that cannot be rushed. A company, similarly, needs time to learn how to work as one cohesive unit. Unfortunately, we did not have the time to reach that level of maturity.

CHAPTER FOURTEEN

THE PARTNERSHIPS THAT DID NOT MATERIALIZE

Throughout its short history, Geotek was involved in an extraordinary amount of strategic partnerships, from the USI merger that kept the company afloat in the early 1990s; to our acquisition of companies such as NB3, Milicom, and GMSI; to our relationships with major corporations such as Mitsubishi, IBM, Hyundai, and Hughes Electronics. There were a few crucial partnerships, however, that never made it into fruition. Each, in its own way, would have involved a major restructuring of Geotek, and, with that, a considerable amount of risk. I believe, however, that if any of these deals had taken place, the company would have become a far stronger one.

During much of the 1990s, the business of reselling wireless service was a fairly substantial one. It worked on a model very similar to the one used by resellers of long-distance telephone service, wherein the reseller buys minutes in bulk from a provider with a physical network and then markets and sells them to customers under its own brand. By the summer of 1996, when I first met Steve Katz, his company, Nationwide Cellular, was the biggest wireless reseller in the country, with

250,000 subscribers, mostly in the Northeast, and annual revenue of $200M. The majority of the company's subscribers were business users, and a substantial minority of these, about eighty thousand, were commercial subscribers that could have benefited from the kind of enhanced services that Geotek was offering. On top of their substantial customer base, Nationwide Cellular also had dozens of sales, support and installation centers in many markets. These too were very attractive to Geotek, as our equivalent facilities were still limited.

Despite Nationwide Cellular's success in attracting high-paying customers, its long-term prospects were bleak, as both Steve Katz and his company's investors understood. In 1996, the major wireless providers were just beginning to make their big push into retail distribution. What had been an industry characterized by complex sales procedures was fast becoming one of the most competitive marketing-intensive sectors of the economy. In this atmosphere, wireless providers were increasingly anxious to take away as much business as possible from their resellers, and the easiest way to do that was to squeeze their margins. As a result, Nationwide Cellular's earnings in 1996 were down to just $8M on $200M in sales, and the company's market-cap hovered around $100M-$150M. Geotek, by way of contrast, was valued at $800M-$1B over the same period, and its earnings were significantly negative.

The idea that emerged as I began talking to Katz was that Geotek would acquire Nationwide Cellular in some sort of a stock deal. Katz brought it up with his company's Board of Directors, which supported investigating the idea further, and began a several-month long process of due diligence that lasted into late 1996. Geotek, meanwhile, began doing its own due diligence, although our board was a little more hesitant than Nationwide Cellular's. The more we looked into the proposed merger, however, the more convinced I became that it made sense. Geotek, after all, had a network in the U.S. but still no subscribers and only a limited human infrastructure. Nationwide Cellular, on the other hand, had everything but a physical network - including a substantial subscriber base. Though there was no guarantee that we could convert their SMR customers to FHMA, a survey we took of these customers showed that they were interested in the type of services GeoNet was planning to offer, including the data applications. I figured that if we managed to entice even just half of the 80,000 relevant Nationwide Cellular business subscribers to switch to GeoNet, it could provide an enormous boost for the new network. At a $1000 in revenue per subscriber per year ($80 a month), which was a reasonable estimate at the time, 40,000 subscribers would translate to $40M in annual revenue, the vast majority of it in profits. Given how undervalued Nationwide Cellular was in relation to the size of its subscriber base, the company could have been an enormously attractive acquisition for Geotek, especially since Katz was asking for only a small premium to the company's then market value.

Unfortunately, the deal with Nationwide Cellular never took place. Partially, this was the result of a failure on Geotek's part (as well as my own) to pursue the opportunity as vigorously as possible. Mostly, however, the plan fizzled because of GeoNet's disappointing premature launch. When Nationwide Cellular's representatives visited our labs and demo sites, the system had always worked. In the field, however, there was no hiding the fact that the technology just was not ready yet. The failure of the launch made Geotek look like a much riskier proposition than it had only months before, so Nationwide Cellular accepted a rival offer instead. The company was acquired, in a deal worth over $200M, by MCI, which was desperate to strengthen its own fledgling cellular resale business.

As disappointed as I was about losing the Nationwide opportunity, I have since come to view it as an even greater loss. I truly believe that had the acquisition taken place, it would have quickly turned Geotek into a very real force in the market for specialized wireless services. I suspect it also would have made it much easier for us to raise the additional capital needed to complete work on GeoNet and achieve a positive cash flow.

One of the biggest issues Geotek struggled with since entering the wireless world was the difficulty of acting as both a technology developer and a service provider. Early on, this duality was a source of pride for the company. I, for one, viewed it more as a strength than a vulnerability, as it gave us a great deal of freedom in controlling our own destiny. We could set our own timetables, design our system to our own specifications, and not have to answer to suppliers many time our size. Furthermore, FHMA was a major differentiator from the rest of the field. By late 1995, however, as we missed our initial target launch date, I was starting to view things differently. It was becoming clear to me that the complexity of doing so many things at once was taking a greater toll on Geotek than I had ever anticipated. The realization came gradually – one day, it was all too clear; the next, we would overcome a major technological hurdle, and I would wonder whether I had not overreacted, whether we might not be able to make it after all. In Europe, the TETRA standard was still in the air, and digital SMR deployment was in its infancy throughout the rest of the world as well. It seemed a shame to lose control of PST's technology at a time when its potential appeared so great. Nevertheless, our main goal had always been to become a service provider, not just another technology start-up.

I continued going back and forth on the question of whether to try to somehow spin off PST throughout 1996, as Geotek frantically raced towards the finish line that was GeoNet's launch. Early that year, our partnership with HNS was at its most promising. They were eager to expand their activities away from the defense market and into the commercial one, and appeared genuinely excited about FHMA and its possibilities. I decided, therefore, to raise with HNS the idea of a merger between them and PST. It was all very preliminary, but the controlling figures at HNS did show some interest. They were conflicted, however, as was I. It was a major commitment about which neither side felt too comfortable. One of the only people at Geotek with whom I discussed the idea was George Calhoun, who had always been my closest advisor on strategic matters. In this case, however, he did not offer me decisive advice. George was even closer to FHMA than I was, and though he understood the need to get its "headaches" out of our way, he was as reluctant as I was about taking such a big step.

A merger between PST and HNS would not have netted Geotek any money. Had it happened, PST would likely have been sold to HNS for just $1, along with a commitment by HNS to continue developing and improving the technology and to supply GeoNet with equipment and services under favorable terms. Nevertheless, it would hardly have been a gift, and HNS understood that. Though they believed in the FHMA technology, they knew it well enough to realize that taking charge of its continued development would be a major challenge. Ultimately, with neither HNS nor Geotek pushing very hard for the merger, the proposal simply fizzled. By the time it became clear to me just how critical it was for us to separate GeoNet from PST, HNS had lost interest. It had already made a number of expensive cellular-related investments that year, and was no longer in the market for any more. In addition, I suspect that working with PST and Rafael for a while had a chilling effect on their desire to enter more deeply into such a complex and difficult project.

A few months before GeoNet's launch, we entered into talks with another promising potential technology partner. The company in question was E.F. Johnson, an over seventy-year-old company, which had once been one of Motorola's biggest rivals. Founded around the same period as its former archrival, the now struggling Minnesota-based RF equipment maker had never made the leap to newer digital technologies. As a result, it had become increasingly marginalized in the wireless industry, with the market for its antiquated, if reliable, private radio technology rapidly shrinking.

The idea of approaching E.F. Johnson started with a conversation I had with Michael Price, a friend of mine and a good Telecom banker with Lazar, who mentioned that a group of investors he knew had recently taken over the company at a rock-bottom price. The main reason I found E.F. Johnson an attractive potential partner for Geotek was that, in spite its not so recent fall from grace, the company still had a very strong brand name. It had carved itself a small niche market in which it was still a major player, and few of its customers (or former customers, for that matter) realized just how small it had become. In 1995, it had only about $100M in sales, mostly to private operators in the US, such as police and fire departments, and to customers in Asia. Much of E.F. Johnson's production had been moved overseas, so by the time I first visited its sprawling headquarters in a small Minnesota town, it had the look and feel of a semi-abandoned factory. Though that did not concern me too much, there were several worrisome issues that did.

The first question we needed to answer was whether it would be possible to develop an FHMA solution to serve E.F. Johnson's core customer base of small local organizations, such as police and fire stations, which needed to run their own basic private radio networks. Though it was a business with little growth prospect, it still accounted for E.F. Johnson's $100M in annual revenue, a significant amount of money by our standards. As it turned out, however, PST quickly came up with an elegant technological solution for making affordable low-capacity FHMA networks. The bigger obstacle to a possible merger, from Geotek's perspective, was E.F. Johnson's management. While we wanted to get the technology off our own backs, it made little sense to hand it over to people we could not trust to handle the responsibility. The problem was that the investors who had acquired the company were much stronger financially than operationally. They had hoped to quickly turn around the company and sell it at a profit, but they had no vision other than cutting costs and pursuing a somewhat more aggressive sales strategy. It was not at all clear to me that they were up to the task of transforming E.F. Johnson into a supplier of advanced digital SMR products.

One crucial element of the merger plan was to bring in an external strategic investor, such as a private equity fund, to invest some money (perhaps about $20M) in the merged company. When I presented the merger idea to Geotek's board, however, I still had not really begun to look for this third party. As a result, the board, which was normally very supportive of my ideas, showed a great deal of concern about this one. Many of the board members saw the merger idea as another one of my attempts at expansion, as a symptom of a kind of megalomania rather than as a strategic vision. In their defense, I had been aggressive in pursuing expansion opportunities throughout most of my tenure at Geotek. My attitude had always been that we could do everything at once: develop technology, build an American network, and grow internationally. This was not the reason I proposed the deal with E.F. Johnson, however. This time, I wanted to make Geotek smaller, not bigger. Unfortunately, I could not convince the board of this, and though they never said "no" to the merger, they made it clear that they did not like the idea. I suspect that if I had been able to find a reputable external investor, the board would have changed its position and supported the merger. As it was, however, with so many other issues on my plate, such as the upcoming GeoNet launch, I did not pursue the matter as diligently as I could have.

There is little doubt in my mind that a merger with E.F. Johnson would have presented Geotek with a whole new set of challenges, and that its success would hardly have been a "sure thing." Nevertheless, I do believe it was the strategically correct move, and that it would have been worth the risk. I view my failure to pursue it more vigorously, therefore, as one of my biggest mistakes at Geotek.

In anticipation of a potential spin-off of Geotek's technology division, we decided, after GeoNet's initial, unsuccessful launch, to make a clear organizational break between the technology division and the rest of the company. To announce the reorganization of the company, we held a special well-attended press conference on the roof of the Park Lane Hotel in New York, overlooking Central Park. As part of that restructuring, we created a new American PST subsidiary, which encompassed not just the Israeli PST but also GMSI and MIS, our data applications companies, as well as our NJ-based technology group. To run the company, I hired Steve Pierce, a former VP from Nortel who made a wonderful impression during his interview but failed miserably at the job. As with several other executives we recruited from large corporations, he could not adapt to working within Geotek's much more fluid, less hierarchical, environment, and lasted in the job only a few months. Ultimately, the changes the reorganization brought about were largely cosmetic. We had hoped it would help jolt sales of FHMA equipment to outside companies, but PST's only customers remained GeoNet and ANAM Telecom in Korea.

CHAPTER FIFTEEN
THE END OF GEOTEK

By the spring of 1997, I had begun to believe that the worst was behind us. Geotek's prospects, in fact, seemed brighter than they had in a long time. We had resolved most of our network problems; sales, though modest, were picking up; and, as a result of January's $130M round of financing, there was still plenty of funds in our bank account. The only cloud on the horizon was the fact that Geotek's stock, which had been trading at just below $10 in the beginning of the year, was losing value week after week, with no end in sight. Given Geotek's positive fundamentals, however, I believed that this was just a temporary setback. In fact, I decided to take advantage of the situation to exercise much of my own stock options, whose prices ranged from $1 to $16. The logic behind the move was that, from a tax perspective, it turned future appreciation of the stock into capital gains profits rather than income. I exercised several hundred thousand options when the stock was trading at around $4. Despite the relatively low value of the share, however, exercising the options was a significant financial commitment, both because of the need to pay Geotek and the taxes on the "paper gain" at the time of the transaction. To pay these costs, I borrowed money from my brokerage account, using the Geotek stock I already owned as collateral.

There was one event during the summer of 1997 that did cause Geotek's share price to spike. We had always known that we would eventually have to replace the Tadiran switches we used to connect calls both within the GeoNet network and to the outside world. Tadiran had done a good job of customizing a large PBX switch to our needs, but to optimize performance of a network as complex as GeoNet, it was clear we needed a far more advanced switch – one built from the ground up to support a mobile network with both push-to-talk and data functionality. Since FHMA was such a new technology, it was hardly surprising that none of the switches available on the market were perfectly suitable for our needs. Regardless of whether we chose to buy from Lucent, Nortel or any other major telecommunications equipment maker, a certain degree of customization would have to be done. The problem was the cost. To the giant vendors in the field, GeoNet was just a tiny potential customer – barely a blip on the radar screen, and certainly not deserving of special discounts. The mobile switches offered by these companies were designed, for the most part, to support metropolitan areas with millions of potential subscribers – something that just was not applicable in our case. Our entire cost calculation was based on spending no more then $50 per subscriber on switching costs. Rather than go with one of the major switch makers, then, we decided to take a different route. We gave the contract to a company with limited previous experience in the field, but an almost legendary record of technological innovation – IBM. They would design a switch for us that was based on an entirely different technology. Instead of a basically analog device, it would be a computerized, or "soft" switch. The idea for this kind of implementation had been around for a while, but no major provider had ever adopted it. We did not save any development money by choosing the IBM solution, but it cemented our reputation as a champion of new and innovative technologies. Even more importantly, the deal included an agreement that IBM would begin reselling GeoNet's services and equipment to their customers. It was an unusual role for IBM, but given their customer base of some of the country's biggest corporations, it certainly had potential.

Though I had expected the market to react positively to the news of our partnership with IBM, I was taken aback by the intensity of the response. Geotek's stock, which traded at around $4 before we announced the deal, jumped rapidly to over $6 on extremely high volumes. It was one of the few times Geotek made the most active list on NASDAQ. In the weeks and months that followed, however, the share price resumed its steady decline.

It was shortly thereafter that this decline began to have a noticeable effect on my own finances. My losses on paper had been significant for several months, of course, but now I was getting margin calls. The reason was simple – I had paid for my exercised stock options using a margin account whose primary asset was the Geotek stocks I already owned. By the time I started receiving the margin calls, however, I did not want to sell my shares – largely for fear it would create an impression that I was "fleeing the ship," which could farther destabilize Geotek. Instead, I increased the mortgage on my house and used the cash to settle the debt. The issue of insiders selling stock was perceived by many in Geotek to be a big issue in the eyes of investors. It was viewed almost as a form of betrayal, though in retrospect, I doubt that my selling stock, as a response to margin calls would have been perceived that negatively by investors. As the stock continued to fall throughout 1997 and early 1998, the margin calls kept coming. To prevent me from having to sell my Geotek shares, the Board of Directors approved giving me a $300K loan. Later on, I received additional loans, totaling over $600K, from CIP (Win Churchill's fund), the Chatterjee Group, and Lenny Klehr, who was Geotek's outside legal counsel as well as a personal friend.

With Geotek's stock price steadily dropping, both the board and I became increasingly concerned that the company could soon face a cash crunch. In the past, we had always been able to count on our ability to raise more capital. Now, however, Geotek's valuation had fallen so low that we simply could not raise the kind of money needed to support our burn rate of over $10M per month. As a stopgap, we turned to a group of investors that cared less about the stock price than about the general viability of the company and the liquidity of its stock – the hedge funds. With Gary Fuhrman's help, we sold them another $30M worth of convertibles, under the same terms as those of the previous transaction. The difference was that this time around, the theoretical number of shares the convertibles corresponded to, relative to the size of the offering, was far greater (since this number is equal to the size of the offering divided by the stock's price). There was no way to know when the hedge funds would convert their convertibles to common shares. All we could do was hope that it would be done when the price of the stock had recovered a little.

~·~

Geotek's 1997 annual shareholder meeting, held late that summer, was a relatively somber affair, in sharp contrast to the more upbeat gatherings of previous years. We held the meeting in a nice but low-key hotel near our corporate headquarters in Montvale, NJ – a more modest venue than the luxurious New York hotels we had used just months earlier for similar high-profile events. It was a reflection of Geotek's emerging financial problems, of course, but also of the fact that we did not want to draw too much attention to ourselves, or to the past year's financial results. Nevertheless, turnout for the meeting was quite high, reflecting, I suspect, both our investors' concerns and a certain degree of cautious hopefulness on their parts. We did have some good news to share by this point – regarding both the technical issues we had solved and the rise in the number and satisfaction level of our subscribers - and I was looking forward to doing so. One of Geotek's board members, Richard Liebhaber, a former Vice Chairman at MCI, brought along a guest to the annual meeting – a consultant by the name of Peter Kim. Later that afternoon, a few of Geotek's top executives and I met with him for what we expected would be a short, routine courtesy meeting. Instead, Kim proceeded to give one of the clearest, most fascinating analyses of strategic product positioning and branding I have ever heard. Hearing him was a revelation – one that could not have come at a more opportune time, as we were just beginning to make plans for the public re-launch of GeoNet. Given our diminishing cash reserves, it was clear that we had precious little room for error this time around. The re-launch just *had* to be a success if Geotek was to survive.

The initial meeting with Peter Kim was followed by several more, each of which involved a growing number of participants from both Geotek and Bright Sun Consulting. Though Kim's firm was only medium-sized, its roster of clients included some of the biggest names in corporate America, such as the oil giant Exxon. Despite this, however, or perhaps because of it, Kim's team grew quite fond of GeoNet and its product. Once an initial proposal was developed by Bright Sun, we hired the firm to design and implement nearly every aspect of our re-launch campaign, which was to be revealed along with a finally-stable handheld phone (we had already begun selling the handhelds in small numbers, but the units were still not production quality). The central theme of the campaign designed by Bright Sun was GeoNet as a network for the "mobile workforce." In some ways, there was nothing very radical about this, as it was a natural extension of our existing marketing strategy. What made the plans unique were their intensity and focus. By late 1997, as many as fifteen Bright Sun staff members were assigned to the Geotek account. The redesign of the GeoNet brand was to encompass everything from changes to products' names and appearances to a new logo for Geotek. It included a major print advertising campaign and an overhaul of all sales literature. Perhaps the most crucial goal of Bright Sun's plans, the goal that was a little radical, was to change the public's perception of GeoNet – from a voice network with some data services as well, to a *communications* network offering a wide variety of targeted applications, of which voice was just the most basic. Years later, it would come to seem like an obvious concept. In 1997, however, it was a risky proposition. While most everyone understood, in a general sort of way, that data was the future for the wireless industry, it still took a leap of faith to make it so central so soon. Part of Peter Kim's brilliance was in understanding that GeoNet needed to commit, truly commit, to what it had been preaching for years. During our first launch, we had paid dearly for offering data applications that were just not ready for mass distribution. Now, the time had come to try to reap the rewards for our efforts.

The problem, unfortunately, was that Geotek was nearly broke. Though we had raised $160M since the beginning of 1997, we were burning about $11M a month on maintaining, supporting and operating GeoNet, as well as on development and production of FHMA equipment.

———·—·—·——

It was only in the early fall that I found out the real reason the price of Geotek's stock was decreasing so steadily. The bearer of the bad news was our CFO, Robert Kirstein, who had replaced Mike McCoy when he had become Geotek's COO and the President of its U.S. network. One day, Kirstein came to my office and told me he had discovered something very strange about Geotek's ownership situation. It appeared, he said, that fully 10% of the total number of outstanding shares were being shorted, an astonishing amount. In the previous few years, the short position in Geotek had been stable at around one million shares. Kirstein's figures indicated that that number had gone up by a factor of ten! Over the succeeding weeks and months, we found out that the vast majority of the sell orders were coming through untraceable offshore brokers' accounts. There was only one logical group of investors that could orchestrate, and profit from, the sale of such an enormous amount of shares at a constantly diminishing price—the hedge funds that had bought into our variable-priced convertible offering. Unlike other investors, the hedge funds owned a financial instrument whose *face value was fixed*. Since the conversion price was a function of Geotek's stock price, the number of stocks a convertible could be redeemed fluctuated inversely to this price. The hedge funds could make a profit at any time by redeeming the convertibles and immediately selling their freshly minted common shares. They could make an even greater profit, however, by first selling shares, and only then converting. It was completely illegal to convert preferred shares to cover short positions but that did not make it any less lucrative. The key was that by selling shares short, the hedge funds would depress the stock's price. Once that had happened, the convertibles would be redeemed for a greater number of shares than had been borrowed. The remaining shares represented pure additional profit. More importantly, they could be sold, along with more borrowed shares, to further reduce the stock's price, and so on ad infinitum. It was, essentially, a reverse pump-and-dump scheme, and it worked so well in Geotek's case because two conditions were met: the hedge funds had the equity to sway the market, and Geotek was a sound enough company that its stock remained liquid even as it fell to record lows. The second convertible offering we had just completed, worth $30M, had only added fuel to the fire.

Clearly, the time had come to take drastic steps. We decided to sell off our non-core assets. The most obvious of these was our majority position in Bogen, which the company's other shareholders agreed to acquire for $18.5M. More painfully, we also sold our European networks, for a total of $107M, the vast majority of which was paid for NB3. Under Geotek's leadership, the European networks had grown substantially, with NB3 becoming Europe's largest "non-cellular" wireless network, with over 100,000 subscribers and strong profits. Though the returns yielded by these deals were quite handsome, they paled in comparison to our operating costs. The proceeds from the sales gave us a little bit of breathing room, but they did not solve our fundamental financial problems, especially since NB3 was one of the assets pledged to our secured bond holders, which meant that we were allowed to use only a portion of the proceeds from the company's sale as working capital. The rest of the funds were placed in a pool of capital available only for infrastructure expenses, much of which was never utilized. Ironically, since Geotek sold its European networks at a huge profit, the company reported a very large capital gain in its financial statement just a few months before filing for Chapter 11 protection. In fact, Geotek's profits for the first quarter of 1998 were so strong that we received our second straight award for being the fastest growing company in New Jersey.

In December 1997, with the Geotek share trading at around $1-$2, I received a call from the office of George Soros, asking me to come for a meeting right away. Though Soros was Geotek's single biggest investor, with over $100M invested, I had met him only socially in the past. All his dealings with Geotek were handled by PC Chatterjee, who seemed to have all but complete discretion in managing Soros's high-risk technology investments. Now, however, with his investment in Geotek all but wiped out, Soros decided it was time to take direct responsibility over it.

The meeting that morning was a long and tense one. To a large extent, Soros was even more upset with his team than with me, especially when he realized the specifics of the preferred convertible financing structure Geotek had employed, with the Board of Directors' unanimous approval. With mounting anger, he counted off the names of long-gone companies that had been devastated by similar financing schemes. As an investor who had famously been on the other side of the shorting equation – albeit legally – he had a keen understanding of the kind of pressure the hedge funds could exert on Geotek's stock. To his credit, however, he spent little time in pointing fingers. A couple of weeks earlier, he had hired a team of two industry veterans to look at all aspects of Geotek's operations and technology. Though I was not privy to these consultants' report, it seemed to have been fairly positive, indicating that the company was doing well in terms of sales and that its customers were satisfied with the solutions being offered to them. Though he was obviously unhappy with the mistakes that had been made, Soros had concluded that Geotek was worth saving. He realized, furthermore, that of Geotek's investors, he was the only one capable of pouring more money into the company. He was willing to invest another $50M, he told me, if several conditions were met: firstly, an industry professional would be appointed to replace me as CEO (I would remain Chairman of the Board); secondly, a work plan for 1998 would be drawn up for his approval; and, thirdly, Geotek would negotiate an agreement with the hedge funds whereby the remaining unconverted convertibles would be exchanged for ones with fixed conversion prices. It was the last of these terms that concerned me, as I knew how little leverage we had over the hedge funds, despite the fact that they had already made back most or all of their investment. To me, this was the most infuriating part of the story – throughout the last months before Geotek filed for bankruptcy, the hedge funds were just "playing" with their profits, even as it was clear that this behavior was destroying the company. They had no interest whatsoever in whether we succeeded or failed in the long term.

The hedge funds, however, were just one piece of the puzzle. As Geotek embarked on a series of increasingly intricate negotiations with its key investors, I realized how big an impediment the company's piecemeal financing structure was. Almost every time a new class of investors had come in, they had been issued new preferred shares. With each new class of stocks, the dependencies and rules of preference grew more numerous and complex. As a result, any fundamental financial restructuring of Geotek now required the agreement of a large number of parties. The most powerful of these were the hedge funds, who had the ability to manipulate the stock as they pleased, and the junk-bond holders, whose bonds were secured by Geotek's physical assets, including the spectrum licenses. Already, we had had to negotiate with the bondholders to sell our European networks. While routine operating expenses were now piling up at an extremely alarming rate, there was still an enormous amount of cash in our bank accounts that accounts payable could not touch, since it was earmarked for infrastructure investments only. In early January, I conducted negotiations with Merrill Lunch, as the bond holders' representative, on allowing us to use some of the proceeds from the sale of NB3 and Bogen for operating expenses. Though the negotiations were long and at times unpleasant, Brian Ison behaved professionally throughout and never lost sight of the big picture. We concluded the discussions after an hour long conference call when I mentioned to Brian that I was speaking from my car with a Geotek phone. Since the quality of the audio was great and the call had not dropped the entire time, Brian felt good enough about Geotek's prospects to make some additional concessions that freed up more cash for operating expenses.

The bond holders' behavior was in stark contrast to that of the hedge funds, which, in their quest for short-terms gains, were systematically, and illegally, using their position of power to destroy the company. It was for this reason that Yoram

Bibring, who had been Geotek's CFO until late 1995, and Robert Vecsler, the company's in-house legal counsel, suggested that we should declare bankruptcy as early as possible. They argued that filing for Chapter Eleven would strengthen the position of Geotek's debt-holders and weaken the position of its equity holders. In particular, the hedge funds would find it much more difficult to manipulate the company's stock under the watchful eye of the bankruptcy court. A new investor, on the other hand, could be given special protections by the same court. While there was much merit to Robert and Yoram's idea, I refused to even consider it, believing that it was much too premature to think in those terms. As the founder of Geotek, and its most prominent public face, I found even the discussion of filing for bankruptcy highly unpleasant, and the whole thing made me angry. Later on, I came to understand that going into bankruptcy while Geotek was relatively strong would have allowed us to get out of it strongly as well. At the time, however, I believed that filing for bankruptcy protection before it was absolutely necessary was defeatist, even "wrong" somehow. By the time Geotek did file for Chapter Eleven, six month later, the company was too weak to effectively fight for survival.

The conflict about whether we should file for Chapter 11 was one of the reasons the period of January to March was so tense. Some of my closest friends on the management team had a very different view from mine on what needed to be done to save the company. Combined with the enormous effort of trying to put together a restructuring plan and, at the same time, maintain positive momentum in the market despite equipment shortages, it made for a very stressful and difficult few months. I spent a great deal of time on the road, speaking to local managers, our sales force, and even large potential customers. My primary preoccupation, however, was the restructuring plan.

There were two key elements to the restructuring plan we tried to "sell" to Geotek's various financial backers. The first was a major financial restructuring, backed by a new infusion of cash from George Soros. The second was the re-launch and re-positioning of GeoNet, which was based on the work we had just recently completed with Bright Sun. I was convinced that the sharp new focus on productivity enhancement for the "mobile workforce" would finally give GeoNet the distinct identity that its unique offerings warranted and establish the network as a true provider of "value-added" services. The clear new positioning was important not only in providing direction to our sales force, I believed, but also in convincing investors that Geotek could position itself in the marketplace vis-à-vis Nextel and the cellular operators.

At times, it seemed like the negotiations with the hedge funds, Chatterjee and Soros, and the various other parties would be successful. After months of intense talks, we had drafts of agreements in place with nearly everyone involved. It was a period of intense work for many of us at Geotek, but we were aided by the fact that the company's results for the final quarter of 1997 and the first few months of 1998 were the strongest they had ever been, with sales topping predictions in most markets. Almost as importantly, the sales figures validated our re-launch plans for GeoNet, as they showed that the majority of our customers were purchasing data plans. Our biggest orders, in fact, often involved integration with customers' enterprise software, as was the case with Airborne Express, which purchased five thousand user subscriptions from us. Other major GeoNet customers included Time Warner Cable, PepsiCo, and Hilton Hotels, to name a few. By the end of the first quarter of 1998, we had about 25,000 users on our network, which was operating commercially in New York, Philadelphia, Boston, Washington DC, Orlando, Miami, Tampa, Dallas, Houston, San Antonio and Phoenix. Our invoicing had reached millions of air-minutes and data packets per month. What made our proposals convincing was the fact that we were able to deliver real value to our customers with services that other wireless carriers simply could not offer. GeoNet's "killer" application was the vehicle location system, which relied on a GPS chip embedded into every phone we produced, and gave fleet managers the ability to monitor their vehicles in real-time.

On a Monday afternoon In March 1998, after almost three month of intense negotiations, I was informed by PC Chatterjee that he and Soros had decided not to invest any more funds in Geotek. They had come to a decision, he said, that giving the hedge funds a fixed conversion price that they would accept would simply dilute the stock too much. Without a new deal with the hedge funds, on the other hand, they viewed Geotek as too risky to finance. It was a devastating blow, especially since I believed that we had come so close to arriving at an agreement. It was particularly hard for me to accept the idea that a company like Geotek could become impossible to finance even though its vision and technology had proven themselves in the marketplace. Since 1994, Chatterjee and Soros had been our most loyal backers, and the fact that they had decided to cut their losses, while certainly understandable, was difficult to take.

Following the meeting with Chatterjee, I decided to consult with William Spier, one of Geotek's board members. I had never liked Spier very much, and I did not think he liked me either, but I did hope he would be willing to help. Although he was not a particularly active director, Spier had had a long career on Wall Street, and I thought he might offer me some fresh ideas. When I told him what had happened earlier, he made a surprising offer. Rather than continue to do everything, he suggested, why don't I hand over to him responsibility for the restructuring and financing efforts. He would become Geotek's Chairman of the Board, while I would continue to serve as the CEO, charged with the continued building the business, including the somewhat muted re-launch. I discussed Spier's suggestion, over the phone from his office, with both Chatterjee and Win Churchill, and though neither was overly enthusiastic about it, they agreed to support whatever decision I made. I decided to accept the offer. I left Spier's office with the hope that together we would be able to find a solution to Geotek's funding problem.

It did not take long before I realized I had made an awful mistake. Part of the problem was Spier's unwavering belief in his own abilities. It soon became clear that he was enamored mainly with the idea of being Chairman of the Board of a highly visible wireless company, and that he was set on making a name for himself as the savior of Geotek. About a month or so prior to his becoming Chairman, I had hired a new CFO, Anne Eisele, whom Spier had worked with before and warmly recommended (her predecessor, Robert Kirstein, had served as Geotek's CFO for less than a year before resigning, stating that the job was too big and stressful for him). Now, Spier and Eisele became the basis of an alliance of new people at Geotek who had an incredible hostile attitude towards me and nearly everyone else who had come before them. They saw me as the cause of the company's problems, and would not accept the fact that I was playing a very critical role in trying to overcome them. Another major figure at Geotek, Deelep Advani, who had been hired by the Chatterjee Group to follow and support the restructuring activities, was also sidelined. This was likely the result of the fact that, in his short time at Geotek, he had become a major promoter of my restructuring and reorganization ideas (at one point in the process, Deelep told me that within weeks we would all know if I was a genius or a mad man pursuing an impossibly ambitious task). Immediately after assuming the role of Chairman, Spier approached Wilber Ross, a well known restructuring expert working for the Rothschild investment bank, an extension of the European Rothschild empire. Every day, it seemed, the trio of Spier, Eisele, and Ross came up with a new model for saving Geotek. They had many variables to play with - the number of markets, the number of base stations per market, cutbacks in staff, ways of exiting markets (brownouts vs. blackouts), and so forth. There was nothing wrong with the models, but Spier and Ross took the reliance on them to an extreme. They completely ignored the important intangibles that could not be modeled, such as the good will, or lack thereof, of the major investors whose agreement we needed for any restructuring plan. The goal was for Rothschild to present their new plan to our major strategic investors and get their support for it. Spier often called for a telephonic board meeting a couple of times a week to present the new ideas with which they had come up. All of these were of little value, and Geotek's investors rejected them without fail.

On a personal level, I was sidelined almost as soon as Spier became Chairman. Though I was still Geotek's CEO, I found myself with little to do, and almost no first-hand knowledge of what was happening with the restructuring efforts. It was an odd situation for me, since for so many years I had been the public face of Geotek and the key person behind important decisions. Now, when investors and colleagues called, I did not know how to answer their questions. My frustration level grew daily as I witnessed the "Spier team" waste critical time and critical investor good will on ridiculous restructuring plans. Spier knew next to nothing about the wireless industry or, for that matter, about running a business. He relied heavily on Eisele, who was a competent technocrat but nothing more, and Richard Krants, a director who had come to Geotek via the Metro Net acquisition, and whose abilities were very limited as he had run only a small business. Even worse was the choice of Rothschild as Geotek's restructuring advisors. The investment bank had virtually no experience, or contacts, in the telecom industry, and Wilbur Ross was utterly unengaged and contributed nothing. His most memorable moment was during a conference call, when he could be heard snoring loudly by participants in multiple locations. Ultimately, the most significant damage caused by Spier was in his alienation of the constituencies on whose good will Geotek's fate rested. In spite of our problems, we still had a good working relationship with Soros and Chatterjee, HNS, Merrill Lynch and Rafael. A deal between those key players, none of whom had an interest in seeing Geotek file for bankruptcy protection, was key to any successful restructuring effort.

I spent most of April and May on the road, talking to employees in the different markets and giving presentations to large potential customers. In April 1998, my wife and children joined me in San Antonio during Passover. It was during this family vacation, as I was receiving calls from New Jersey informing me of changes about which neither I nor the board had been consulted, that I started to realize that I had lost the ability to impact the fate of Geotek.

In April 1998, only a few weeks after Bill Spier became Chairman of the Board, PC Chatterjee, Win Churchill and I agreed that we should ask him to resign. We decided the request should come from Chatterjee, who represented our biggest investor. A few hours after the two spoke, I received a call from an Spier, who, spewing obscenities, informed me that he would accept our request and tender his formal resignation during Geotek's next board meeting, scheduled for early the following week. In agreeing to resign, he suggested that his leaving would spell the end of Geotek – a shocking statement given that he had been serving as Chairman for a few weeks, with little in the way of results to show for it. Though Spier and I had never been especially close, I had known and worked with him since the early 1990s, and was surprised and mystified by the extent of his deluded rage.

Geotek's next board meeting took place in a stifling room at the Manhattan office of our accountants, Cooper and Librant. To the surprise of nearly everyone there, Spier informed us that he had decided not to resign. It almost felt as though he was trying to egg the board into a confrontation. If we wanted him out, he seemed to be saying, we would have to fire him. This was surprising as Spier did not have a big investment in Geotek or represent anyone who did; his move was driven by ego and nothing else. The meeting quickly degenerated into informal discussions, held by small groups of directors out in the hallway. It dragged on for hours, as many board members waited for responses from advisors and superiors, some of whom were not immediately available to take calls. In the end, however, it became clear that the group that wanted Spier replaced by me was outnumbered, though just barely, by Spier's supporters. We never called for a formal vote, but an informal tally showed that four directors: Win Churchill, PC Chatterjee,

Walter Auch, and I, supported firing Spier. Five were against. The most bruising aspect of the vote was the decision by George Calhoun, one of my closest advisors since 1991, to side with Spier. It was a betrayal, and though I never believed George's reasons were personal, I do view his vote as a symptom of his weaknesses as an executive. Ultimately, he chose to take the easy way out. We remained friends, but the sting of what happened that day has never completely evaporated.

Shortly after that turbulent board meeting, Win, Chatterjee and Auch resigned from the board, saying that a potential bankruptcy filing might hurt their standing with some large pension funds that they were working with. I considered resigning as well, but was advised against it by my lawyer. Despite the fact that I was nominally Geotek's CEO, I soon became almost entirely cut off from the decision making processes at the company. At Spier's request, I stopped coming to the office on a regular basis, arriving only for the occasional meeting in which my presence was still required. I also continued to attend board meetings, which were being held very frequently, but remained largely silent. With those directors who had supported Spier's ouster no longer there, the board was dominated by members who wanted to see my "era" of Geotek over. For over a month, I had little to do professionally, with neither an office to go to nor an assignment to pursue. Finally, in June, Spier asked for my resignation. In this last conversation with me, he was as petty and mean-spirited as he had been for months, suggesting that if I left quietly and without arguing Geotek would not sue me. I was never clear what I had done to warrant such a suit, but Spier seemed to think it was a terribly potent threat. As it was, I had little desire to stay anymore. That Sunday, I went to the office with my wife, Hagar, cleared out my desk, and left seven years of very hard work behind.

I had been with Geotek, in one incarnation or another, for virtually my entire professional career. Now, for the first time since my days at Wharton, I was without a job.

—◟•◞—

The "Spier team," which lost the cooperation of all of Geotek's major stakeholders, failed to produce any kind of resolution to the company's problems. In August 1998, five month after I left the driver's seat, the company filed for Chapter 11 bankruptcy protection. In the months that followed, its assets were sold under court supervision. The sale generated about $250M, which was used to pay back all the secured creditors and most of the unsecured ones. As expected, the shareholders got nothing. Our dream of bringing the most innovative wireless technology to millions of commercial customers was over.

CHAPTER SIXTEEN
CONCLUSIONS

For all the press coverage that Geotek received over the years, in both the American and Israeli media, its story was never well understood. As is so often the case with ambitious, visionary, and thus volatile ventures, it was viewed in black and white terms. When the outlook was good, we could do no wrong, and when conditions suddenly took a turn for the worse, we could do no right. In fact, neither was the case. Geotek had some great triumphs, but it also made grievous mistakes. For all these mistakes, however, I am also convinced that there was a strong element of timing and bad luck to the company's downfall. We ran out of money at the worse possible time, when the market for our products was just about to explode but our capital structure would not allow us to raise more funds. Still, the mistakes we made *were* ultimately our undoing, and had we not made them, Geotek's fate might have been very different.

Our first mistake was failing to devise a realistic capitalization plan. It took a long time for me to accept that Geotek would need hundreds of millions of dollars to develop its technology and build a network. Even then, I was wary of going to potential investors and asking for that kind of money.

Instead, we took a piecemeal approach to financing Geotek, raising relatively small amounts of money on many occasions. The result was that the company slowly developed an extremely cumbersome capital structure. By late 1997, we had fifteen distinct classes of preferred stock and three classes of debt. Since Geotek was born a public company, spun-off from Patlex, we could not raise money with a traditional Initial Public Offering (IPO). We could, however, had done a secondary public offering. We chose not to largely because easier methods were available to us. When the company was doing well, this was of little significance, but when the cash crunch of 1997-1998 came, it had a detrimental effect on our ability to negotiate a restructuring of the company. Preferred shareholders, by their very nature, have privileges that common shareholders do not. As a result, there were just too many parties that had a seat at the table during the restructuring negotiations. In hindsight, I believe that, regardless of whether we had chosen to raise money from preferred or "common" investors, we should have been far more direct about our long-term capital needs. Geotek's vision was appealing enough that it might well have been possible for the company to raise the capital it needed in fewer rounds of financing, freeing us from the need to constantly worry about the stock's price, or to dabble with such risky instruments as preferred, variable-priced convertibles.

The second critical reason for Geotek's failure was the complexity of its operations. Simply put, we tried to do way too much. In the 1980s, Motorola tried to be both a technology provider and a private radio network operator. By early the following decade, it had decided it could not effectively do both, and proceeded to sell off its network business. If

Motorola could not pull it off, what chance did we have? FHMA did provide a way for us to enter the wireless world, but there was no way we could succeed as a technology developer once we also had to contend with the enormous challenges of running a commercial network. In 1995-1996, we had a couple opportunities to transfer the technology business to other companies, namely HNS and E.F. Johnson. We did not take these opportunities. I suspect that if we had, though, Geotek would have been easier to finance and more likely to succeed.

There was one other area in which crucial mistakes, many of them my own, were made – the choice of people for important positions at Geotek. When we first entered the wireless business, I hired a young management team with little experience in that field, but a lot of enthusiasm, motivation and intelligence. Geotek was their company, and they cared about it a great deal. In mid 1995, I decided that the time had come to bring in some "professionals" from the industry, ones with more experience in network deployment, wireless service sales and customer support. The transition was not beneficial to Geotek. Many of the people I hired had strong skills but did not care the way the "old guard" did. They came from large corporations and were often unwilling, or unable, to adjust to Geotek's more informal, less hierarchical, culture. The knowledge and experience they brought to the company proved far less valuable than the energy and commitment of the group of executives who ran Geotek in the earlier years. I am sure that during the difficult days of 1997 and 1998, Geotek would have been much better off with a different blend of experience and heart among its top executives.

On a personal level, running Geotek remains the defining experience of my professional life. It was an incredible rollercoaster ride, and the positive memories from that time far outweigh the negative ones. As painful as Geotek's demise was, the fact that there was so much to lose was ultimately a testament to just how much had been built. I remember telling my wife, Hagar, in 1990, that if I could not quickly raise $250,000, the company would be unable to pay its employees. I could never have imagined back then that in seven years Geotek would be on the verge of collapse because it had "only" $50M in the bank and was "burning" $11M a month. By that point, we had 1200 employees and were paying rent for hundreds of towers, T1 communication lines, and vehicles worldwide. I felt like a captain of a jet plane who had discovered a malfunction seconds before taking off. There was no way to safely slow down anymore, and only two bad options remained – to try to make it to cruising altitude, or to turn around and risk never being able to get off the ground again. I had lots of power but almost no flexibility. As an entrepreneur, the thought of giving up so late in the game was anathema to me. I could feel the window of opportunity closing, so I decided to do everything in my power to get through the takeoff. There were moments when I truly believed we would make it, but, in the end, it just did not happen.

The years after Geotek were not at all easy for me. When Spier had called to demand my resignation, he had made sure to note that I would not be receiving any severance pay. With $2M in debts and few savings, I had little choice but to recover as soon as I possibly could. The day after resigning, I showed up at a small office building in Wayne, NJ to start Selway, a holding company jointly owned by myself and Boaz Raam, who also owned the office building. I did not know if after all the turmoil at Geotek I would be accepted by the world around me as a venture capital investor. Lenny Klehr, a good friend of mine who had been Geotek's outside counsel, gave me one piece of advice when I told him about my new career plan. He told me that in my new line of work I would run into two types of people: those who appreciated what I had accomplished with Geotek and would be willing to work with me, and those who did not. His advice was that I focus on the former group. It was a simple, even obvious, suggestion, but a very useful one too, and I have followed it ever since.

The last six years have been good to me. Selway has grown into a successful incubator of technology start-up companies, and I was later invited to join SCP Private Equity Partners, the firm started by Win Churchill, as a partner. As a professional investor, I now receive many proposals for technology companies. I have yet to see any, however, whose vision is as unique and pioneering as was Geotek's. The flip side, of course, is that the proposed companies are not nearly as complex either.

GLOSSARY

CDMA – Code Division Multiple Access

COO – Chief Operation Officer

CEO – Chief Executive Officer

FDMA – Frequency Division Multiple Access

FHMA – Frequency Hopping Multiple Access

Fuze – An ignition device of a bomb or shell

HNS – Hughes Network Systems

iDEN – Integrated Digital Enhanced Network

Sectorization – RF transmission using directional antennas

SKD – Semi Knockdown

SMR – Specialized Mobile Radio

TDMA – Time Division Multiple Access